A Guide to Irish Military Heritage

I0892104

Maynooth Research Guides for Irish Local History

GENERAL EDITOR Mary Ann Lyons

This book is one of the Maynooth Research Guides for Irish Local History series. Written by specialists in the relevant fields, these volumes are designed to provide historians, and specifically those interested in local history, with practical advice regarding the consultation of specific collections of historical material, thereby enabling them to conduct independent research in a competent and thorough manner. In each volume, a brief history of the relevant institutions is provided and the principal primary sources are identified and critically evaluated, with specific reference to their usefulness to the local historian. Readers receive step by step guidance as to how to conduct their research and are alerted to some of the problems which they might encounter in working with particular collections. Possible avenues for research are suggested and relevant secondary works are also recommended.

The General Editor acknowledges the assistance of both Dr Raymond Gillespie, Co-ordinator of the M.A. in Local History Programme, N.U.I. Maynooth and Dr James Kelly, St Patrick's College, Drumcondra, in the preparation of this book for publication.

IN THIS SERIES

Terence A.M. Dooley, *Sources for the history of landed estates in Ireland* (Irish Academic Press, 2000)

Raymond Refaussé, *Church of Ireland records* (Irish Academic Press, 2000)

Patrick J. Corish and David C. Sheehy, *Records of the Irish Catholic Church* (Irish Academic Press, 2001)

Philomena Connolly, *Medieval record sources* (Four Courts Press, 2002)

E. Margaret Crawford, *Counting the people: a survey of the Irish censuses, 1813–1911* (Four Courts Press, 2003).

Brian Gurrin, *Pre-census sources for Irish demography* (Four Courts Press, 2002).

B. Hanley, *A guide to Irish military heritage* (Four Courts Press, 2004)

Maynooth Research Guides for Irish Local History: Number 7

A Guide to Irish Military Heritage

EDITED BY

Brian Hanley

FOUR COURTS PRESS

This book was set
in 10.5 on 13.5 Times Roman.
Published in Ireland by
FOUR COURTS PRESS LTD
7 Malpas Street, Dublin 8, Ireland
e-mail: info@four-courts-press.ie
http:\\www.four-courts-press.ie
and in North America by
FOUR COURTS PRESS
c/o ISBS, 920 N.E. 58th Avenue, Suite 300, Portland, OR 97213.

© Military Heritage of Ireland Trust Ltd 2004

A catalogue record for this title
is available from the British Library.

ISBN 1–85182–788–9 hbk
1–85182–789–7 pbk

All rights reserved. No part of this publication may be reproduced, stored in or introduced into a retrieval system, or transmitted, in any form or by any means (electronic, mechanical, photocopying, recording or otherwise), without the prior written permission of both the copyright owner and publisher of this book.

Printed in Great Britain by
MPG Books, Bodmin, Cornwall.

Contents

Illustrations

(Illustrations appear between pages 64 and 65.)

CREDITS

7 Cashman Collection, Military Archives, Cathal Brugha Barracks, Rathmines, Dublin; 5, 6, 9, 10, 12 Military Archives, Cathal Brugha Barracks, Rathmines; 1 National Museum of Ireland; 2, 3, 4, 8, 11 The Royal Ulster Rifles Museum, Belfast.

Acknowledgments

This is the seventh volume in the Maynooth research guides for Irish local history series. In several important respects it differs in format and content from previous pamphlets in the series. Unlike earlier volumes that explore the research potential of particular classes of records, such as landed estate collections, Church records and census material, this guide focuses on a particular historical problem, namely, how one should approach researching a history of the involvement of Irish men and women in military campaigns at home and overseas. While it outlines some of the challenges associated with researching specific campaigns or the careers of particular individuals, the primary aim of the pamphlet is to provide detailed, practical guidance regarding the location and consultation of a wide range of documentary, oral and material sources, held in a variety of repositories throughout Ireland and, to a lesser extent, Britain.

Mary Ann Lyons, series editor

Compiling this guide would have been impossible without the generous assistance of archivists and librarians. Particular thanks must go to Commandant Victor Laing and the staff at Military Archives, Dublin, Caitriona Crowe at the National Archives, Labhrás Joye at the National Museum, Collins Barracks, and Seamus Helferty at UCD Archives. Less personal, but no less genuine thanks are also due to all those who sent valuable information to the project. Throughout the course of compiling the guide I was greatly assisted by Professor Eunan O'Halpin. I must also thank the directors of the Military Heritage of Ireland Trust, and Richard Doherty for their help, particularly in editing the manuscript. John Paul Ryan also assisted in many ways. Finally many thanks to the staff at Four Courts Press for their usual efficiency.

The material in the guide was collected in January 2003; it has been adjusted in December for changes brought to our attention.

Brian Hanley

The development of this guide
was supported by

THE IRELAND FUND.

Abbreviations

DMP	Dublin Metropolitan Police
DOD	Department of Defence
GAA	Gaelic Athletic Association
ICA	Irish Citizen Army
IRA	Irish Republican Army
IRB	Irish Republican Brotherhood
IRFU	Irish Rugby Football Union
LDF	Local Defence Force
NLI	National Library of Ireland
NUI	National University of Ireland
PRONI	Public Record Office of Northern Ireland
RAF	Royal Air Force
RIC	Royal Irish Constabulary
RUR	Royal Ulster Rifles
TCD	Trinity College Dublin
UCC	University College Cork
UCD	University College Dublin
UCG	University College Galway
UN	United Nations
UVF	Ulster Volunteer Force

Introduction

This guide is designed to help those doing research into aspects of Irish military history from earliest times to the present day, whether they are seeking information on a family member's participation in an historical conflict or engaged on a course of academic study. It was commissioned by the Military Heritage of Ireland Trust Limited which was established in June 2000 to foster knowledge of Ireland's military heritage, and its relationship to the economic, political, social and cultural life of the country.

This guide aims to fill a definite need. There is a significant level of interest in the remembrance and commemoration of Irish participation in warfare; but many people are unaware of how to locate sources on the subject. This short book explains the steps to be taken when seeking information on military history; it lists the institutions, archives, public bodies and organizations that hold information relevant to military heritage, and it provides brief descriptions of the material held by them.

Because the Military Heritage of Ireland Trust is eager to record military heritage in its broadest sense, museums, fortifications, battle sites and places in Ireland relevant to military affairs are included.

The world-wide web being a major resource for those embarking on research, a section is devoted to web-sites relevant to Irish military history; where possible, it is indicated whether a website is that of an institution or official body, or the work of an enthusiast, which *may* be less authoritative.

Very often, a researcher's questions will at least be partially answered by published work; therefore an up-to-date bibliography is provided.

One of the major aims of the Military Heritage of Ireland Trust is to promote an inclusive view of the Irish men and women who participated in conflict, but unfortunately it has not always been possible to do this. Commemoration and remembrance have often been embroiled in controversy, with the result that the military service of many Irish people has been effectively forgotten. This guide attempts to promote the study of all Irish military participation, regardless of location or the cause espoused. In the twentieth century alone, for example, Irish men and women have fought in two world wars, on both sides in the Boer War, the Spanish Civil War and in a revolution and civil war in Ireland itself. The guide identifies sources for the study of all these conflicts as well as for the Irish Defence Forces and the armed services of the United Kingdom.

Not everyone seeking information will be satisfied. Firstly, a much greater volume of material exists for the twentieth century than for earlier periods. Therefore it will be more difficult to find archival material on warfare in the Middle Ages than in First World War. Even when researching quite recent conflicts, problems may still arise, as in the case of those seeking information on a relative's service. Much important material on the role of the Irish in the British armed services is held in Britain. It is also an unfortunate fact that it will be easier to find information on someone killed in either of the two world wars than on a person who served but survived. In many cases, files will be released only to proven next-of-kin or with the permission of the individual's family. It is advisable to gather as much information as possible on an individual before commencing archival research as this greatly improves the chances of being successful. Research on the revolutionary period in Ireland presents particular problems. For example, we still have no complete record of the dead from the 1916–23 period. Thousands of Irish people served in revolutionary or non-state military formations, and for a variety of reasons, records of these movements are incomplete, scattered, or hard to access for the non-academic researcher. Where possible, are signalled particular problems or restrictions that may confront a researcher.

How to use this book

BEGINNING RESEARCH

Preliminary research into local military history will often begin at one's local public library; therefore a complete list of local libraries has been included in this guide. For more detailed information, however, it will usually be necessary to visit one or more specialist archives. The major repositories for Irish military records are the Military Archives, the National Archives of Ireland, the National Library of Ireland, University College Dublin Archives (all in Dublin), the Public Record Office of Northern Ireland (Belfast), and the National Archives (in London). Many archives of schools, religious bodies or private companies also hold relevant records.

ARCHIVAL RESEARCH

Before visiting an archive, it is usually necessary to phone, write or e-mail the archivist to arrange an appointment. Archives are often subject to restrictions of space and resources, and staff cannot be expected to conduct research on behalf of members of the public. Each archive has rules for researchers which are outlined on one's first visit. Researchers are not allowed to use pens or biros in most archives, so it is advisable to bring a pencil and paper; most archives now also allow readers to use laptop computers. You will generally not be allowed to bring personal belongings into the archives proper. Archives are often extremely busy, so be prepared for occasional delays and remember that the staff are often under considerable pressure. The documents that you consult must be treated carefully and with respect, for in many cases they are old, unique and irreplaceable. You may be able to order photocopies of documents, though it can take some time for orders to be processed and a charge usually applies.

TELEPHONE & FAX NUMBERS

The numbers given in this Guide include
the local area code but *not* any international prefix.

TRACING AN INDIVIDUAL'S RECORD

A researcher interested in an Irish person who served in the armed forces of Ireland (since 1922), or of the United Kingdom, or of the USA, Australia or Canada at any time since the late nineteenth century, has a reasonable chance of finding relevant information in libraries, state archives and on the world-wide web. In general, however, the earlier the dates in question, the less chance there is of finding material (this is because state and military record-keeping acquired a modern character only around 1900). Before embarking on a search, it is important to gather as much information as possible of the following: the person's name, date of birth, area of origin, and details of the unit or regiment in which he or she served (no information for the twentieth century is available without the person's service number, in the case of UK, US, Canadian, Australian or New Zealand forces).

When researching the Irish Defence Forces, one's starting point should be the Military Archives at Cathal Brugha Barracks, Dublin. However, in most cases detailed information will only be supplied to a proven next-of-kin. For details of pension records, write to Veterans' Allowance Section, Department of Defence, Renmore, Galway; this also applies to veterans of the 1916–23 period. The Medals files, detailing the recipients of medals for service from 1916 to 1921, are held in Cathal Brugha Barracks and are accessible to proven next-of-kin. For access to personnel records of non-commissioned officers and other ranks, write to Other Ranks Administration, Defence Forces HQ, Parkgate, Dublin 8. For commissioned officers from Second Lieutenant upwards, write to Officers' Administration, Defence Forces HQ, Parkgate, Dublin 8.

Gaining access to information on a relative who took part in the War of Independence or the Civil War can be more difficult. In this regard, the researcher is directed to the Collins papers that deal with various aspects of organization of the Irish Volunteers, Irish Republican Army (IRA) and the National Army from 1913 to 1922. This collection is stored in the Military Archives. Over 1,700 witness statements of veterans, recorded by the Bureau of Military History, are now also accessible at Cathal Brugha Barracks.

Those who served in the National Army after 1922 were awarded pensions through the Army Pensions Act of 1923. Those who fought on the anti-Treaty side in the Civil War became entitled to pensions under the 1934 Military Service Pensions Act. These records can be accessed through the Veterans Allowance Section, DOD, Renmore, Galway. However, it should be noted that a number of anti-Treaty veterans refused to apply for either medals or pensions. If a researcher is focusing on the National Army, the complete army census of November 1922 can be consulted at the Military Archives; records of anti-Treaty internees are also held there.

Details of those who served in the Local Defence Forces during the Emergency are recorded in the Local Defence Force files and rolls, both of which are held by the Military Archives. Sources on Irish participation in United Nations peacekeeping operations are also stored there. Service in the pre-1916 Irish Volunteers, Cumann na mBan, the Citizen Army and the IRA after 1919 can be traced through consulting a variety of collections held in diverse institutions. While there is no guarantee of success in isolating a particular individual's record, there are strong possibilities of discovering more about activities in a particular area. Major historical resources for the 1916–23 period are held at UCD Archives in Dublin. Among these are the papers of revolutionaries such as Sean Mac Eoin, Richard Mulcahy, The O'Rahilly, Ernie O'Malley, Moss Twomey, and Sighle Humphreys. The Mac Eoin and Mulcahy collections contain much valuable information on the organization of the Irish Army after 1922. The archive also holds over 350 interviews with veterans of the period conducted by Ernie O'Malley, as well as separate collections of documents relating to the Irish Volunteers. Information on post-1922 Army re-organization and Irish Army Intelligence work can be found in the papers of Colonel Dan Bryan.

Many documents relevant to this period, including material on the Ulster Volunteer Force (UVF) and the IRA in Ulster, are also available at the Public Record Office of Northern Ireland (PRONI). Among these are the papers of Ulster Volunteers organizers General Sir George Richardson and Colonel Fred Crawford; county-by-county records of the UVF; and memoirs of the Larne gunrunning. The files on republican prisoners interned after 1922 are also now open to the public. Tracing twentieth-century service in the British armed forces is, in some respects, an easier task. Information on a relative killed in either the First or Second World War, be it in British or Commonwealth service, can be accessed by post or online, at Commonwealth War Graves Commission, 2 Marlow Road, Maidenhead,

Berkshire SL6 7D. Tel: 0044 1628 634221 Web http://www.cwgc.org. By consulting the CWGC's 'Debt of Honour' register, one should be able to trace a relative who died in either world war. The register lists the names of 1.7 million members of the British and Commonwealth forces who died in both world wars and those of over 60,000 British civilians who died in World War Two. It is useful to have details of an individual's regiment and year of death if possible. Pre-1914 British Army service records are held at the National Archives, Ruskin Avenue, Kew, Richmond, Surrey TW9 4DU. Tel: 0044 20 8392 5200.

The National Archives, London, has also made available service records for First World War soldiers and non-commissioned officers, although many were lost through bombing during the Second World War. For details of these, check http://www.pro.gov.uk/research/easyreach/army-otherranks-wwlletters.htm London's Imperial War Museum has published a series of excellent guides to tracing service in the British Army, Royal Navy, Royal Air Force and Merchant Navy. These are available from Family History at the Imperial War Museum, Lambeth Road, London SE1 6HZ. Tel: 0044 20 7416 5320 E-mail mail@iwm.org.uk The United Kingdom's Ministry of Defence holds records for soldiers who served after 1922 until the mid 1990s. These are available from the Army Records Centre, 26 Bourne Avenue, Hayes, Middlesex UB3 1RF. The ARC will release records to proven next-of-kin for a fee (currently £25) and there may be a lengthy wait for this service.

Researching the career of an individual who served before the twentieth century is more difficult. However, there are still quite extensive records for the organization of yeomanry and county militias within Ireland. Militia and yeomanry lists for Antrim, Armagh, Down, Fermanagh, Londonderry and Tyrone from the 1600s onwards are held at PRONI. Other sources, including material on the United Irishmen and the 1798 Rebellion, can be checked at PRONI's Records of Military Interest. British military history from 1485 to the present time is the preserve of the National Army Museum in London, Royal Hospital Road, Chelsea, London SW3 4HT. Tel: 0044 20 7730 0717 Web http://www.national-army-museum.ac.uk

The National Archives of Ireland hold the 1798 Rebellion papers, the 1803 Rebellion papers and the State of the Country papers from 1790 to 1830, which contain widespread material of military interest. Here you will also find information on yeomanry and militias, court martial reports and intelligence notes on organizations such as the Fenians.

Archival collections

Allen Library

Edmund Rice House, North Richmond Street, Dublin 1. Tel: 01 8551077 Fax: 01 855 5243 E-mail allenlib@connect.ie Web www.allenlibrary.com

This repository houses an extensive collection of leaflets, posters, correspondence, press cutting, photographs and memorabilia including medals, relating mainly to the 1916–23 period. It also contains material relevant to the Irish Volunteers, the Irish Republican Brotherhood, Cumann na mBan, the Irish Citizen Army and the IRA down to the conclusion of the Civil War. Correspondence between, or reference to, numerous personalities involved in the Independence struggle, both well-known figures such as Collins and de Valera and more obscure local activists, is also available. There is a smaller amount of material related to the Fenians and the 1798 Rebellion, and to the Defence Forces during the Emergency (the Second World War years). The collection also contains information on the German bombing of Dublin's North Strand during 1941.

Open 10.00am–4.00pm, Mon.–Fri.; by appointment. Restricted photocopying available.

Birr Castle

The Estate Office, Ross Row, Birr, County Offaly. Tel: 0509 20023 Fax: 0509 20425

The archives contain the papers of Admiral Sir Edward Hawke, first lord of the admiralty (1766–71), and material relating to the 1798 Rebellion in the papers of Sir Laurence Parsons.

Access restricted.

Boole Library, National University of Ireland, Cork

Tel: 021 4903180 Fax: 021 4273428 E-mail c.quinn@ucc.ie Web www.booleweb.ie

A number of collections here have material of military interest. The Grehan family papers include letters and diaries of Major Stephen Grehan who

served with the British Army in France during World War One. The Ryan of Inch papers contain letters (1782–1802) relating to the military career of Major Denis MulRyan in the service of the Austrian emperor. Also in this collection are log-books of voyages in the service of the Royal Navy by John F. Ryan between 1870 and 1879. Furthermore, there is a collection of papers relating to Thomas MacDonagh, the executed 1916 leader, although it features little of military interest. The Peters photographic collection contains photographs taken by Major C.M.D. Peters while he was with the American First Army during the invasion of Germany in 1944–5. Among the collection are photographs of the liberation of Buchenwald concentration camp in 1945.
Access by appointment.

Castle Matrix
Rathkeale, County Limerick. Tel: 069 64284
Formerly the headquarters of the International Institute of Military History, Castle Matrix stores papers relating to the service of the Irish in French and Spanish armies during the 1700s and more recent material dealing with war in the air during World War Two. The castle library holds a number of volumes of military interest, particularly relating to the Wild Geese; it is open to the public from June until August (11.00am–4.00pm).
Access by appointment.

Church of Ireland, Representative Church Body Library
Braemor Park, Churchtown, Dublin 14. Tel: 01 4923979 E-mail library@ireland.anglican.org
This is the principal theological and reference library of the Church of Ireland, with over 40,000 volumes in its collection. It is also the principal repository for the Church of Ireland's archives.
Open 9.30am–1.00pm, 2.00pm–5.00pm, Mon.–Fri.

Communist Party of Ireland Archives
Connolly House, 43 East Essex Street, Dublin 2. Tel: 01 6711943
The CPI are in the process of cataloguing and preserving their archives which will contain material of relevance to the 1916–23 period and the participation of Irish volunteers on the republican side during the Spanish Civil War. As yet it is not accessible to researchers.

Cork Archives Institute
Christ Church, South Main Street, Cork. Tel: 021 4277809 Fax: 021 4274668
E-mail cai@indigo.ie Web http://www.corkcorp.ie/facilities.archive.html
The Institute holds a number of important collections covering the 1916–23 period, particularly as related to Cork. These include the papers of republican activists Daniel Corkery, Seamus Fitzgerald, Donal Hales, Roibeard Langford, J.J. Walsh, Siobhan Lankford, Terence MacSwiney and Liam de Roiste. There are also miscellaneous items of interest from the revolutionary period scattered throughout other papers. A number of collections such as the Edward Murphy diaries and the Murphy emigrant letters contain material on the participation of Cork men in the British armed forces.
Open 10.00am–1.00pm, 2.30pm–5.00pm, Tues.–Fri. By appointment.

Cork Public Museum
FitzGerald Park, Mardyke, Cork. Tel: 021 4270679 Fax: 021 4270931
E-mail museum@corkcorp.ie
The museum holds a number of collections relating to the War of Independence period such as the Tom Daly and Michael Leahy papers. A recent accession has been the correspondence of Michael Collins and Kitty Kiernan.
Open 11.00am–1.00pm, 2.15pm–5.00pm, Mon.–Fri.; 3.00pm–5.00pm, Sun.

Derry Diocesan Archive
9 Steelstown Road, Derry BT48 8EU. Tel: 028 71359809
The archive contains a limited body of material relating to the presence of British and United States forces in Derry during the Second World War and afterwards.
Access by appointment.

Derry City Council Heritage and Museum Service
Harbour Museum, Harbour Square, Derry BT48 6AF. Tel: 028 71377331
Fax: 028 71377633 E-mail tower.museum@derrycity.gov.uk
Among the records of Derry City Council and Londonderry Corporation are files relating to the use of Eglinton Airport by Coastal Command, Fighter Command and the Fleet Air Arm from April 1941. The base was used to help escort convoys in the north Atlantic, to defend the northwest from air attack and to train air crew. The archives also contain the four-volume City of Londonderry War Memorial Records.
Access by appointment.

Dublin City Archives
138–142 Pearse Street, Dublin 2. Tel: 01 6744800
E-mail cityarchives@ dublincorp.ie
The archives contain some information on employees of Dublin Corporation who took part in the First World War and the 1916 Rising. Records relating to the German bombing of Dublin's North Strand in 1941 are also held here.
Access by appointment.

Franciscan Library and Archives
Dún Mhuire, Seafield Road, Killiney, County Dublin. Tel: 01 2826760
The archives hold the Wadding papers which cover the period of the Catholic Confederation of Kilkenny, founded in the aftermath of the 1641 Rebellion. However, access to these papers is severely restricted.

Gaelic Athletic Association Museum
New Cusack Stand, Croke Park, Dublin 3. Tel: 01 8558176 Fax: 01 8558104
E-mail gaamuseum@crokepark Web www.gaa.ie/museum/
The museum houses a new archive with a growing collection but as yet it is of value for specialist rather than general research. A limited number of materials pertaining to the relationship between the GAA and the nationalist movement in the early twentieth century are accessible on request. These include the records of the military inquiry into the Bloody Sunday massacre, 1920.
Access by appointment.

Garda Siochána Museum and Archives
The Records Tower, Dublin Castle, Dublin 2. Tel: 01 6719597
Web www.esatclear.ie/~garda/index.html
The archives contain documents relating to the history of the Royal Irish Constabulary and the Dublin Metropolitan Police, some of which pertain to the conflicts from 1916 to 1923.
Access by appointment.

Guinness Archives
Guinness Storehouse, St James's Gate, Dublin 8. Tel: 01 4714557 Fax: 01 408473 E-mail guinness.archives@guinness.com
More than 800 employees of Guinness joined the British forces during the First World War, and over 100 were killed. The archives contain extensive reports on employees held as PoWs and on food parcels sent to them, as

well as on pensions for invalided former employees and allowances to families of servicemen. A commemorative roll of Guinness employees who died in the British Army, Royal Navy and Royal Flying Corps as well as several files on those who served are available, as are records relating to the Boer War, the involvement of workers from the company in the 1916 Rising, the War of Independence and the Civil War, and on the impact of these conflicts on the company's affairs. The archives also include records of leave granted to employees serving in the Defence Forces during the Emergency.
Open 9.30am–5.00pm, Mon.–Thur.; 9.30am–4.30pm, Fri. Access by appointment. Personnel records generally only accessible by relatives.

Irish Jesuit Archives
35 Lower Leeson Street, Dublin 2. Tel: 01 6761248
The archives contain a number of records relevant to warfare in Ireland. Among these are the MacErlean transcripts, which cover the years from 1527 to 1774 and include documents relating to Jesuit involvement in the Baltinglass revolt, the Nine Years War and the Williamite War. There are also a number of diaries of Jesuit chaplains who served with British regiments in both world wars. The First World War photographs of Fr Browne SJ, who served with the Irish Guards and was awarded the Military Cross, are held at Gonzaga College, Sandford Road, Dublin 6.
Access by appointment.

Irish Labour History Museum and Archives
Beggars Bush, Haddington Road, Dublin 4. Tel: 01 6681071 E-mail ilhm@dna.ie
The ILHS Archives contain a limited amount of records of relevance to military history. These include an Irish Citizen Army minute book, 1919–20, and memoirs of Irish volunteers for the Spanish Republic. The papers of trade unionist Cathal O'Shannon feature references to his career as a member of the Irish Republican Brotherhood and the Irish Volunteers and to the role of labour in the War of Independence and the Civil War.
Access by appointment.

Irish Rugby Football Union
62 Lansdowne Road, Dublin 4. Tel: 01 2852023
Seventeen Irish rugby international players died in the First and Second World

Wars. From the Boer War onwards, over thirty were decorated for their wartime service. The IRFU hold a number of books which record their sacrifice, including *The Rugby Internationals Roll of Honour* (1919). The IRFU also has a large collection of national and club histories that contain information of military interest. Some of this material is also available in public libraries.
Access by appointment.

Kilmainham Gaol Museum
Inchicore Road, Dublin 8. Tel: 01 4535984 Fax: 01 4532037
As well as its museum (see separate entry), the gaol's archive contains over 8,000 books, letters, periodicals, legal documents, medals, uniforms and weapons relating to the gaol's history from 1796. The main collections pertain to the rebellions of 1798, 1803, 1848, 1867 and 1916, the Land War of the 1880s, the War of Independence, 1919–21, the Civil War, 1922–23 and the Emergency, 1939–45. Among its holdings are autograph books belonging to prisoners detained between 1916 and 1923 and many of the last letters written by the executed 1916 leaders. The weapons collection includes a pike used by rebels in both 1798 and 1867 and displayed again on parade by Irish Volunteers in 1914.
Access to the archive is by appointment only.

Limerick City Museum (The Jim Kemmy Municipal Museum)
Castle Lane, Nicholas Street, Limerick. Tel: 061 417826
E-mail lwalsh@limerickcity.ie
The museum holds a list of members of the Limerick county militia from 1803 to 1813.
Access by appointment.

Military Archives
Cathal Brugha Barracks, Rathmines, Dublin 6. Tel: 01 4975499/8046457
Fax: 01 8046237 Web http://www.military.ie/military_archives/index.html and (Bureau of Military History) http://www.military.ie/military_archives/bureau_of_military_history.html
The Military Archives are the official archives of the Irish Defence Forces and the Department of Defence. They contain extensive sources for the study of twentieth-century Irish military history. The War of Independence period is covered by the Collins papers, 1913–22. These papers also contain material on the organization of the 1916 Rising, including gun-running

and the attempted recruitment of an Irish brigade from Irish PoWs in Germany. Nationwide reports on the reorganization of the Irish Volunteers after 1917 are available. From 1919 onwards there are reports of IRA operations, Crown Forces' casualties, arrests, imprisonments and executions. Also relevant to this period are the Medals files, containing the applications for 1916 and War of Independence service medals (which are available to next-of-kin or relatives only). A further collection of great importance to the study of the 1913–21 period is the **Bureau of Military History**, 1913–21, papers; these were opened to researchers in March 2003. The Bureau was established in 1947 to assemble and organize material on the history of the struggle for independence from 1913 onwards. Over a ten-year period, more than 1,700 witness statements, 300 sets of contemporary documents, twelve voice recordings, a collection of press cuttings and 200 photographs were collected. Those interviewed include veterans of the Irish Volunteers, Citizen Army, Hibernian Rifles, IRA and Cumann na mBan, as well as political and labour activists. A very useful publication entitled *Introduction to the Bureau of Military History* is available at the Archives.

There are numerous sources for the study of the formation of the National Army and the course of the Civil War. There is also an abundance of intelligence documents on Civil War operations, captured anti-Treaty documents, registers of Army phone and radio communications and collections on the organization of the Special Infantry Corps and the Railway Protection Corps. The returns of the National Army census of November 1922 that detailed every member of the new National Army are also accessible. In addition, the internment records of captured anti-Treaty activists can be consulted. Files for the 1920s cover the organization of the new army, its training and arming, the takeover and occupation of former British barracks, the demobilization process after the Civil War as well as the attempted army mutiny of 1924. Reports on army strengths, movement of units and organization, 1924–39. The military mission to the United States in 1926–7 and the formation of the Air Corps are also covered by separate files. Other files relate to the Volunteer Reserve of the Defence Forces from 1934. For the Emergency period of 1939–45, the archives hold the G2 Irish Military Intelligence Files containing information on Axis and Allied espionage, attempts by the IRA and other groups to enlist Axis support and related matters. Separate collections relate to crashes and forced landings of Allied and Axis aircraft in the state (in which over 220 foreign airmen lost their lives), and to the internment of Allied and Axis personnel at the Curragh Camp in County Kildare.

Separate files cover the internment of IRA suspects and other subversive groups at the Curragh and at Arbour Hill, Dublin. Other collections deal with the Defence Forces' organization and Emergency defence plans, including sets of maps, and air raid precautions and the establishment of coastal defence artillery and the Army Construction Corps. There are files and membership rolls for the Local Defence Forces and reports on German bombing raids on Dublin, Wexford and elsewhere in neutral Ireland. Other files deal with the control of censorship in the state. Material on Irish United Nations participation from 1958 onwards, in the Lebanon, then Congo, Cyprus, Sinai, the Lebanon again during the 1970s and 1980s, Western Sahara and Namibia etc. until the present day is also available.

The Archives also hold collections of journals such as *An t-Oglach*, *An Cosantóir*, army handbooks and training manuals as well as a small library. There are a number of Unit histories involving UN service, a collection of press cuttings relating to the Defence Forces since 1922, and over 850 private collections of papers and documents donated by serving or retired members of the Defence Forces and their families. It is important to note that many of these files, particularly those relating to intelligence, are subject to restricted access. Files on internees are generally only open to next-of-kin or relatives.

Access to the Archives is by appointment only.

National Archives

Bishop Street, Dublin 8. Tel: 01 4072300 Fax: 01 4072333 E-mail mail@nationalarchives.ie Web http://www.nationalarchives.ie/

There are several major collections relating to military history in the National Archives. The Rebellion Papers covering the period from 1790 to 1808 are a major source for the 1798 and 1803 rebellions. These include reports and correspondence from military personnel and government informers, statements from prisoners, letters by government officials and private letters from citizens to the administration in Dublin Castle. They are accessible by card index. Information on barracks and military establishments, as well as residual material of military interest is contained in the State of the Country papers that cover the 1790–1830 period and are listed by county. The Chief Secretary's Office registered papers, which span the years 1818 to 1922, are a rich source, featuring numerous references to local militias and army organization. Unfortunately the catalogue to this collection dates from the 19th century; there is as yet no separate index for entries relating

to military matters. The records of the Royal Hospital Kilmainham contain information on invalided soldiers, particularly from the Crimean War. There are miscellaneous volumes of material dealing with the Longford militia, 1791–1860 and the Sligo militia, 1855–7. The Fenian Papers are an extensive collection of police intelligence reports on that movement, including the 1867 rebellion. A collection of photographs of Fenian suspects is also accessible. The Crime Branch special files contain information on the Irish Republican Brotherhood and other revolutionary bodies from 1887 to 1907. Maintenance details of Royal Irish Constabulary and British Army barracks are included in the Office of Public Works files. Relevant collections relating to the period from 1916 onwards include the Chief Secretary's Office registered papers on 1916, card indexes of 1916 internees and a card index of hunger strikers during the War of Independence period. The files of Dáil Éireann, 1919–1921 also obviously contain relevant material. All legislation dealing with the Defence Forces from 1922 onwards features in the files of the Department of the Taoiseach. These include army reports from 1922 to 1924, reports on the conduct of the Civil War, the enquiry into the 1924 army mutiny, plans for national defence during the Emergency period, the various Military Service Pensions Acts and papers relating to the establishment of a Volunteer Reserve Force. From March 2003, over 1,700 witness statements from the Bureau of Military History may also be consulted at the National Archives and an index to these statements is available there. The files of the Committee on Claims of British Ex-Servicemen from 1927 to1928 covers the demands of First World War veterans for improvements in housing and unemployment relief. They include numerous testimonies from veterans and British Legion branches throughout the Free State. Matters pertaining to the post-Civil War IRA, the Blueshirts and other military bodies are covered in the Department of Justice Jus 8 series of files.
Open 10.00am–5.00pm, Mon.–Fri. Photocopying available. Access with reader's ticket only.

National Library of Ireland Manuscripts
2–3 Kildare Street, Dublin 2. Tel: 01 6766690 E-mail info@nli.ie Web http://www.nli.ie/Default.htm
The NLI's collection includes almost 70,000 catalogued manuscripts. These range from extensive collections of documents to postcards, press cuttings and scrapbooks. As there are literally thousands of items of military inter-

est in these collections, it is advisable to have a clear objective before beginning a search. A useful guide to part of the collection is R.J. Hayes (ed.), *Manuscript Sources for the History of Irish Civilisation* and its supplement, available in the NLI manuscripts room. Later collections may be accessible on the computer catalogue. Searches by name or by subject such as Ireland-History-Rebellion of 1641; Napoleonic Wars, 1800–1812-participation, Irish; South African War, 1899–1902-Participation, Irish; or World War, 1914–1918, Ireland, will yield *some* results. A number of the larger collections also have detailed catalogues in hard copy. Among the main collections related to Irish military heritage are the Kilmainham papers (377 volumes dating from 1780 to 1890), detailing recruitment, supplies, and the movement of troops in Ireland, compiled by various commanders-in-chief. The Wolfe Tone and Lennox/FitzGerald/Campbell papers contain major material of interest to the 1798 Rebellion. The papers of major nineteenth-century political personalities in Ireland such as Daniel O'Connell and William O'Brien all contain some material of relevance. In the case of O'Connell, there is documentation on Irish involvement in the wars of liberation in South America. The James Jordan collection is largely devoted to Irish involvement in the American Civil War. The NLI also holds extensive collections on the 1916 Rising, the War of Independence and the Civil War. Among the most important are the papers of Piaras Beaslai and Florence O'Donoghue, which detail the activities of the IRB, the IRA and the development of the National Army. Also important are the Joseph McGarrity, Ginger O'Connell, Eoin O'Duffy, Erskine Childers, Sean T. O'Kelly, Sheehy Skeffington, Eoin MacNeill and Bulmer Hobson collections. The papers of the former director of the library, Richard J. Hayes, include material on his code-breaking work for Military Intelligence during World War Two.

Open 10.00am–8.30pm, Mon.–Wed.; 10.00am–4.30pm, Thur.–Fri.; 10.00am–12.30pm, Sat.

Admission with reader's ticket issued through the National Library.

National Photographic Archive

Meeting House Square, Temple Bar, Dublin 2. Tel: 01 6030371 Fax: 01 6777451 E-mail photoarchive@nli.ie Web http://www.nli.ie

The archive contains over 300,000 photographs, with a number of collections of relevance to military heritage. The Keogh collection covers the years 1914–23 and includes images of the Irish Volunteers, National Volunteers, Irish Citizen Army, British Army, IRA and National Army. It

also features images of numerous individuals involved in the War of Independence and Civil War. The Valentine postcard collection and the J.W. O'Neill collection deal with the 1916 Rising and its aftermath. The Hogan/Lennon collection has a substantial number of photographs of events from 1920 to 1924, especially during the Civil War. Smaller collections relating to the Civil War are those of Fitzelle, MacConnoran and Matthews. There are also some photographs of interest in the Casement and Sheehy Skeffington collections.
Open 10.00am–5.00pm, Mon.–Fri.; 10.00am–2.00pm, Sat.

National University of Ireland, Cork College Archives
University Heritage Office, University College Cork. Tel: 021 4903552 Fax: 021 4903555 E-mail heritage@ucc.ie
In the Queen's College Cork correspondence (1845–1918) there are letters to and from students who joined the British armed services, especially during World War One. The *University College Cork Official Gazette* (1911–20) contains lists of students who served with the British forces during the First World War. The lists are arranged under the headings of (1) Army, (2) Naval medical service, (3) Royal Army Medical Corps, (4) Indian Medical Corps, (5) Members of staff and (6) Those who applied for commissions. There is some information on the War Guild, a body comprised of the wives of staff members and female students which supported members of Irish regiments at the front and PoWs in Germany. The archives also hold a copy of the *War Record of University College Cork*, published in 1919.
Access by appointment.

National University of Ireland Galway, James Hardiman Library
NUI Galway. Tel: 091 524411 ext 2540 Fax: 091 522394 E-mail www.library.nuigalway.ie/
Among this library's collections, several relate to military affairs, including the papers of Frank J. Carty, officer commanding the IRA's 4th Brigade of the 3rd Western Division, 1919–23. There is also a small collection of papers relating to the murder of two Loughnane brothers at Gort, County Galway, by the RIC Auxiliaries in November 1920. The papers relating to Professor Cillian Ó Briolcháin's service with the Local Defence Force in Galway during the Emergency contain information on training and on defence plans for the Galway area. In the Lucan papers there is a sub-group concerning the career of Charles, third earl of Lucan. These include mate-

rial on the 17th Lancers and the earl's service in the Crimean War. There is also some material relating to military manoeuvres in the frontier provinces of India in 1858. A second set of papers deals with the career of Charles, fifth earl, in the Rifle Brigade, during the period 1881–96, the London Volunteer Corps from 1901 and service with the 1st London Infantry Brigade in Malta and Egypt during World War One.
Access by appointment.

National University of Ireland Maynooth, Russell Library
Maynooth, County Kildare. Tel: 01 7083890 Fax: 01 6286008 E-mail Russell.Library@may.ie Web www.may.ie/library
The library holds the archives of the Irish colleges in Spain, 1619–1871, in which one finds occasional items of military interest.
Access by appointment.

Public Record Office of Northern Ireland
66 Balmoral Avenue, Belfast BT9 6NY. Tel: 028 90255905 E-mail proni@dcalni.gov.uk Web http://proni.nics.gov.uk
There are numerous sources for Irish military history held at PRONI, among them diaries, photographs, official and personal correspondence and press cuttings. Under the Wars and Campaigns index there are entries for the Elizabethan Wars (1594–1603), the Cromwellian War (1649–54) and Williamite War (1688–91), the Wars of the Spanish (1701–14) and Austrian succession (1740–8), the American Revolution (1775–83), the Napoleonic Wars (1793–1815), the Greek War of Independence, the First Burmese War, the US-Mexican War (1846–8), the Crimean War (1853–6), the Indian Mutiny (1857–8), the Nepal War,the American Civil War (1860–5), the Franco-Prussian War, the Ashanti War, the Sudan campaign, the Spanish-American War, the Russio-Japanese War, the First and Second Boer Wars, World Wars One and Two, the War of Independence, the Irish Civil War and the Spanish Civil War. There are further entries under the Rebellions and Insurrections index. As might be imagined, the richness of the collections varies considerably. Among the most important are those which deal with the organization of the militia and yeomanry from the 1600s, the Volunteer movement of the 1780s and 1790s, and the United Irish rebellion of 1798. There are, for example, militia, yeomanry lists and muster rolls for Antrim, Armagh, Down, Fermanagh, Londonderry and Tyrone; regular army muster rolls from the 1630s to the 1830s; files on United Irish activity in County Down from

1797 to 1798; and membership books of the United Irishmen in County Antrim. A large number of letters and diaries from soldiers, sailors, airmen and nurses (usually from Ulster backgrounds) serving in the First and Second World Wars are also available. Records of the Royal Irish Fusiliers, 1914–18 and 1939–45, naval log books from the Dardanelles campaign during 1915 and soldiers' letters describing the battle of Ypres in 1914 are accessible, as are Sir Oliver Nugent's 36th (Ulster) Division papers,1915–24, a volume of press obituaries of Irish soldiers killed in the First World War, and photographs taken by members of the Royal Garrison Artillery in France during that conflict. War diaries and letters from the Second World War include those of United States servicemen based in Northern Ireland. There are also substantial bodies of material relating to the experience of the home front in Northern Ireland, especially during the Belfast Blitz of 1941. Government reports on the hardship caused by the German air raids and diaries and accounts of air raid wardens and members of the Home Guard may also be consulted. The domestic conflicts in Ireland, beginning with the Home Rule crisis, are well covered. The papers of Ulster Volunteer Force (UVF) leaders General Sir George Richardson and Colonel Fred Crawford provide much information on the organization of that body from 1913. PRONI also holds county by county reports on the UVF, papers of its youth section from 1913 to 1915, orders to drivers taking part in the Larne gun-running of 1914, and personal memoirs of participants. The violence of the period from 1919 to 1923 is recorded in police and government reports on the IRA, and there is an alphabetical index of every internee held during those years. Their files are now available to the public. Further records of military interest are contained in various family papers such as those of the Harts from the Derry/Donegal border, one of whom, General George Vaughan Hart, commanded British troops in the American War of Independence, and the Leslies, from County Monaghan, several of whom served in the county militia and in the Crimea and India. A list of these papers is accessible via the web at http://proni.nics.gov.uk/records/military.htm

Open 9.15am–4.45pm, Mon.–Fri.; 10.00am–8.45pm Thur. Photocopying available. First-time visitors must bring identification.

Radio Telefís Éireann (RTÉ) Video and Sound Archives

Donnybrook, Dublin 4. Tel: 01 2083111 Fax: 01 2083080

These archives contain thousands of recordings of radio and television programmes produced by RTE. Access for researchers can be granted and in some cases, copies of programmes made available. Researchers should apply in writing, giving as many details about requests as possible.

The Inniskillings Museum
Enniskillen Castle, Castle Barracks, Enniskillen, County Fermanagh BT74 7HL. Tel: 028 6632 3142 Fax: 028 6632 0359
The museum holds a collection of war diaries and archival material relating to the Royal Inniskilling Fusiliers and 5th Royal Inniskilling Dragoon Guards, which is available to researchers by appointment.
Open 2.00pm–5.00pm, Wed.–Sat., or by prior appointment.

The Royal Irish Fusiliers Museum
Sovereign's House, Mall East, Armagh, BT61 9DL. Tel: 028 3752 2911 E-mail Rylirfusiliermus@cs.com Web www.rirfus-museum.freeserve.co.uk
As well as the Regimental museum, the archives are accessible to researchers, by appointment.
Open 10.00am–12.30pm, 1.00pm–4.00pm, Mon.–Fri.

The Royal Ulster Rifles Museum
5 Waring Street, Belfast BT1 2EW. Tel: 028 9023 2086 E-mail rurmuseum@yahoo.co.uk Web http://rurmuseum.tripod.com
Archival material, such as record books and casualty lists, is available to researchers but permission must first be sought.
Open 10.00am–12.30pm, 2.00pm–4.00pm, Mon.–Thur. (closes at 3.00pm on Fri.). Admission free.

The Somme Heritage Centre
233 Bangor Road, Newtownards, County Down, BT23 7PH. Tel: 028 47823202 E-mail Sommeassociation@dnet.co.uk Web www.irishsoldier.org
The centre holds over 5,000 separate artefacts relating to the First World War. These include letters, postcards, official documents, diaries, pay books, message books and certificates. As well as detailing the experience of the front line soldier, these documents relate to nursing, the home front, and to the Home Rule crisis in Ireland from 1912 to 1914.

Tomás Ó Fiaich Memorial Library & Archive
15 Moy Road, Armagh, BT61 7LY. Tel: 028 37522981 Fax: 028 37511944 E-mail ofiaichlibrary@btinternet.com

The archive holds the Micheline Kerney Walsh Overseas Archive, which contains over 200,000 papers related to Irish emigrés on the Continent. These include military and naval records of descendants of Irish families such as the O'Neills, O'Donnells and Butlers. Among them are the family papers of General Alfredo Kindelan, a former commander of the Spanish Air Force and descendant of chieftains from Meath, and the duke of Tetuán, a direct descendant of Red Hugh O'Donnell. The collection is heavily biased in favour of Spain and France, but material on the Irish elsewhere in Europe, especially Italy (with information on the Battalion of St Patrick), also features. The archive holds an extensive collection of material relating to the War of Independence and the Civil War in the Fr O'Kane papers, which have not been catalogued and are not accessible to researchers at present. The Ó Fiaich Library contains over 15,000 books, with many related to Irish history.
Access by appointment.

Trinity College Dublin Library, Manuscripts Department
Long Room, TCD, Dublin 2. Tel: 01 6081189 Fax: 01 6082690
E-mail mscripts@tcd.ie Web www.tcd.ie/Library/
Among the material of interest to military historians are miscellaneous manuscripts relating to the activities of two foremost Gaelic lords, Shane and Hugh O'Neill, the sieges of Limerick in 1642 and 1651, inquiries into the Desmond Rebellion of 1584 and the Ulster Rebellion of 1615 and numerous military lists from the 1600 onwards. The latter include material on militias and yeomanry in Antrim, Leitrim and Armagh. These and all pre-1900 material can be checked through consulting the *Catalogue of the Manuscripts in the Library of Trinity College, Dublin*. More substantial collections include: the 1641 depositions; the papers of Sir Robert and Edward Southwell (which include material on the Cromwellian war effort in Ireland); the papers of George Clarke, secretary for war, 1690–2, which cover the Williamite War; court martial reports from the 1798 Rebellion; the records of the Trinity Volunteers, 1797–8, as well as substantial material on the United Irish movement in Major Henry C. Sirr's papers and the Thomas Russell collection. There are also the records of the Dublin University Officer Training Corps from the period 1910 to 1922 and a substantial collection on the university's role during the 1916 Rising. The papers of Patrick Pearse, Erskine Childers and Frank Gallagher provide information on the revolutionary period.
Open 10.00am–5.00pm, Mon.–Fri.; 10.00am–1.00pm, Sat.
Reader's ticket necessary.

University College Dublin Archives

Archives Department, UCD, Belfield, Dublin 4. Tel: 01 7167555 E-mail archives@ucd.ie Web http://www.ucd.ie/~archives/

This repository is of immense significance for the study of Irish military history during the twentieth century, especially the revolutionary period 1916–23. Sources for the organization of the Irish Volunteers, Irish Republican Brotherhood, and the 1916 Rising include the papers of Ernest Blythe, Martin Conlon, Cowan family, Desmond FitzGerald, Peter Paul Galligan, Sighle Humphreys, Mary MacSwiney, Sean MacEntee, Eoin MacNeill, Denis McCullough, The O'Rahilly, Bernard O'Rourke, James Ryan and Desmond Ryan. The Cowan and Desmond Ryan papers also provide information on the Irish Citizen Army. Attempts to form an Irish brigade in Germany are covered in the Boehm/Casement and Michael Boyle McKeogh papers. Important material on the Cumann na mBan organization from 1913 onwards exists in the Eithne Coyle O'Donnell, Humphreys, MacSwiney and Lily O'Brennan papers. The post-1916 period and the IRA during the War of Independence are exceptionally well covered in the Frank Aiken, Todd Andrews, Kevin Barry, Caitlin Brugha, Burke Family, Thomas Cardiff, FitzGerald, Humphreys, Sean MacEoin, Con Moloney, Richard Mulcahy, Daniel Mulvihill and Ernie O'Malley papers and notebooks. Sources on the Civil War from an anti-Treaty IRA perspective are contained in the papers of Aiken, Andrews, Burke, Coyle O'Donnell, Humphreys, MacSwiney, MacEntee, O'Malley, O'Rahilly, Ryan and Moss Twomey. The pro-Treaty side and the organization and development of the National Army are well served by the Dan Bryan, FitzGerald, MacEoin and Mulcahy papers. Much of the material contained in specific collections would be useful to local studies; for example, the Longford region features in the MacEoin papers. Many memoirs are contained in Military Service pension applications, especially in the Aiken, MacEoin and Humphreys collections. More general sources on the study of Irish military history are included in the Bryan and Desmond Ryan papers. Material on service in the British and Commonwealth forces are contained in the Cowan family, Tom Kettle, Michael J. Moynihan, Roberts and Company and George O'Callaghan papers. There is also a limited amount of information on service with the Irish Defence Forces during the Emergency in the Andrews, Cardiff and Conlon papers as well as material on intelligence in the Bryan collection. The index to the archive's 'Small Collections' also identifies numerous items of military interest. Most of the larger collections are available on micro-

film, but some of the smaller ones are only available in hard copy and must be ordered in advance.
Access is strictly by appointment. Reader's ticket necessary.
Open 10.00am–1.00pm & 2.00pm–5.00pm, Mon.–Thur.

University of Ulster Library, Coleraine
Coleraine, County Derry BT52 1SA. Tel: 028 70324345 E-mail fj.reynolds@ulst.ac.uk Web www.ulst.ac.uk/library/lib/col.htm
The archives contain the Headlam-Morley collection, which deals with World War One and the Paul Richard collection relating to World War Two. Denis Johnston's papers contain material on his work as a war correspondent in North Africa, the Balkans, Italy and Germany during World War Two. The Francis Stuart collection includes some diaries written during the novelist's time as a broadcaster for the Nazis during the Second World War.

Battlefields, castles, heritage sites and museums

VISITING MUSEUMS AND HERITAGE SITES: BASIC TIPS

The Irish countryside is dotted with sites relevant to military history. Most castles in Ireland were built by the Anglo-Normans with a military purpose in mind, and over the centuries many were subject to attack and siege. From the early 1800s, the coastline was fortified with numerous Martello towers, some of which still exist. The British Army occupied barracks in most Irish towns until 1922, many of which are still visible today, if not always in military use. While all these buildings are of interest in terms of military history, not all are accessible, for a variety of reasons. Restrictions on access apply to museums, castles and heritage sites. Many sites of historic battles may now be at least partly under private ownership and therefore not open to the public. Numerous castles are now ruined and have no facilities for visitors, and permission may be needed to visit them. Some military museums have particular security requirements. A great many local museums are maintained on a voluntary basis and have restricted opening hours and limited facilities. Some of the heritage sites and museums listed below place a heavy emphasis on military history, but others have comparatively little material of military interest in their collections. This guide presents a broad outline of each institution's holdings. It is highly recommended that the opening hours, entrance fees (if any) and rules and regulations for these institutions be checked before visiting. It should be noted that many castles have limited access for the disabled. Almost every town in Ireland has a memorial to local people's service in conflict, whether in the First or Second World Wars, the War of Independence, the Civil War or other conflicts. These memorials are too numerous to list here, but they too bear testimony to the impact of war on Irish society and will be of interest to anyone reading this publication.

Ballymoney Museum
33 Charlotte Street, Ballymoney, BT53 6AY. Tel: 028 27662280 x 245
E-mail keith.beattie@ballymoney.gov.uk
Museum of local history.

Belfast City and Milltown Cemeteries
Information from An Culturlann, 216 Falls Road, Belfast. Tel: 028 90239303 Fax: 028 90964189 E-mail cultur@iol.ie Web www.westbelfast-failte.com
These cemeteries bear testimony to the involvement of Belfast men and women in both world wars and to victims of the Belfast Blitz. Evidence of the conflicts of the 1912–23 period as well as the era from 1969 to the present can be seen in both cemeteries. Milltown contains the city's Republican plot. Tours are available by request, except from 3 to 12 Aug. when they are conducted on a daily basis.

Carrickfergus Castle
Seafront, Carrickfergus, County Antrim. Tel: 028 93351273 E-mail sc@doeni.gov.uk
Constructed in the late twelfth century by John de Courcy, the Anglo-Norman conqueror of east Ulster, this castle was a military stronghold for almost 600 years. It sustained a long siege by Edward Bruce in 1315–16. For several hundred years it was the crown's principal residential and administrative stronghold in the north. It was seized by General Schomberg on behalf of King William in 1689 and was captured briefly by the French in 1760. It functioned as a prison during the Napoleonic Wars, then an armoury until 1928 and later an air raid shelter during the Second World War.
Open to the public. Admission charge.

Dunluce Castle
87 Dunluce Road, Bushmills, County Antrim. Tel: 028 20731938 E-mail sc@doeni.gov.uk
Built on a spectacular viewing point, the castle was a stronghold of the McDonnells, the lords of Antrim during the 1500s. After a siege by Sir John Perott, the lord deputy, in 1584, the McDonnells submitted to Queen

Elizabeth I. The *Girona,* an Armada ship, sank nearby and its cannon were salvaged for Dunluce's defence.
Open Apr.–Sept. Guided tours available. Admission charge.

Dunseverick Museum
Dunseverick Harbour, Bushmills, County Antrim. Tel: 028 20762225
The museum includes exhibits on the Spanish Armada and World War One.

Fernhill House People's Museum
Glencairn Park, Belfast. Tel: 028 90715599
This museum is dedicated to recounting the social, economic and military history of the Greater Shankill area of Belfast. It features various exhibits on the Home Rule crisis and the First World War. The museum also offers a service that traces the First and Second World War records of local people.
Open 10.00am–4.00pm, Mon.–Sat.; 1.00pm–4.00pm, Sun.

Irish Linen Centre and Lisburn Museum
Market Square, Lisburn, County Antrim. Tel: 028 9266377 Fax: 028 92672624 E-mail irishlinencentre@lisburn.gov.uk
A section of the museum deals with the military history of the region.
Open 9.30am–5.00pm, Mon.–Sat.

Langford Lodge Wartime Centre
Station 597, Gortnagallon Road, Langford Lodge, Ardmore, County Antrim. Tel: 028 94423896
During the Second World War the Langford Lodge estate, owned by the Pakenham family, was used by the United States as a major aircraft repair depot run by the Lockheed Overseas Corporations and the 8th Air Force Service Command, US Army Air Force. An aviation museum here contains collections of material relating to air warfare in both world wars and in the modern age.
Open May–Oct. 12.30pm–4.00pm, Sat. & Sun.

The Police Museum
PSNI HQ, 'Brooklyn', Knock Road, Belfast BT5 6LE Tel: 028 90650222 x 22499 E-mail museum@psni.police.uk Web http://www.psni.police.uk/museum/index.htm
The museum houses uniforms, weapons and information on the history of policing in Ireland from 1822, with particular relevance to the Royal Irish

Constabulary in the 1916–21 period. A complete database of RIC service records is accessible at the museum, as well as material on Harbour Police, Belfast Borough Police, the RUC, PSNI and Ulster Special Constabulary.
Open 9.30am–12.30pm, 1.30pm–4.30pm, Mon.–Fri. Visits by appointment preferred.

The Royal Irish Regiment Museum
St Patrick's Barracks, Ballymena, County Antrim. Tel: 028 25661355 E-mail hrirish@royalirishregiment.co.uk
The current Royal Irish Regiment was formed by the amalgamation of the Royal Irish Rangers and the Ulster Defence Regiment in 1992. The original regiment had been formed in 1684 and was disbanded in 1922. Exhibits detail the origins of the regiment with the raising of the Inniskillings in 1689 and include weapons and uniforms. The history of the Irish infantry regiments to the present day is also outlined. The Royal Irish is the last Irish infantry regiment of the line in the British Army.
Open 2.00pm–5.00pm, Wed.–Sat., or by appointment.

The Royal Ulster Rifles Museum
5 Waring Street, Belfast BT1 2EW. Tel: 028 90232086 E-mail rurmuseum@yahoo.co.uk Web http://rurmuseum.tripod.com
This museum holds collections of uniforms, medals, badges, diaries and photographs relating to the history of this regiment, which bore the name Royal Irish Rifles until it was changed to Royal Ulster Rifles on 1 January 1921. There are over 4,000 items in a collection which covers service from Egypt in 1801, through India in 1857, the Boer War, the First and Second World Wars and Korea.
Open 10.00am–12.30pm, 2.00pm–4.00pm, Mon–Thur. (closes at 3.00pm on Fri.) Admission free.

Ulster Museum
Botanic Gardens, Belfast BT9 5AB. Tel: 028 90383000
The Ulster Museum houses collections relating to the arts, natural sciences and history. Periodically it stages exhibitions of military interest, with topics including medieval arms and armour or the local experience of the First World War. The museum also holds material salvaged from the wreck of Spanish Armada ships off the Irish coast (1588).
Open 10.00am–5.00pm, Mon.–Fri.; 1.00pm–5.00pm, Sat.; 2.00pm–5.00pm, Sun.

U.S. Rangers Centre

Boneybefore, Carrickfergus, Carrickfergus Borough Council, Wilson Endowed Building, 15 Lancastrian Street, Carrickfergus, BT 38 7AB. Tel: 028 93366455 E-mail hrankin.tourism@carrickfergus.org Web http://www.carrickfergus.org

The 1st Battalion of the elite US Army Rangers was raised on 19 June 1942 at Sunnylands Camp, Carrickfergus. This museum contains photographs, memorabilia and records relating to this famous unit. It is housed in the same building as the Andrew Jackson Centre, which commemorates the life of Andrew Jackson, major general in the Tennessee militia, victor of the battle of New Orleans in 1815 and seventh president of the United States.

Open Apr.–Oct., 10.00am–1.00pm, 2.00pm–4.00pm. (Open by request for schools and groups during the winter months.) Admission charge.

War Memorial Building

9–13 Waring Street, Belfast BT 1 2DW. Tel: 028 90320392 Web http://rurmuseum.tripod.com/homefront.htm

This building is located on a site devastated by German bombing in 1941. A permanent exhibition entitled *Northern Ireland in the Second World War* details the social, economic and military background to the region's involvement in that conflict.

Open 9.00am–5.00pm, Mon.–Fri. Admission free.

ARMAGH

Armagh County Museum

The Mall East, Armagh, BT61 9BE. Tel: 028 37523070 Fax: 028 37522631 Web www.armagh-visit.com/county_museum.htm

This museum has on display important collections of objects relating to the Tyrone, Louth and Armagh militia; the Irish Volunteers, yeomanry and Royal Irish Fusiliers. It also holds weapons including pikes used in the 1798 Rebellion and a range of materials dating from the two world wars. The museum library contains a number of lists of army men and royal marines, and yeomanry from the early nineteenth century.

Open 10.00am–5.00pm, Mon.–Fri.; 10.00am–1.00pm, Sat. Admission free.

Benburb Valley Heritage Centre

89 Milltown Road, Tullymore, Benburb, County Armagh. Tel: 028 37549885

This heritage centre is close to the site of the June 1646 battle where Gaelic forces under the command of Eoghan Roe O'Neill defeated Scottish troops under Robert Munroe. The biggest battle of the eleven-year Confederate War, some historians have described it as the only pitched battle the Gaelic Irish ever won.

Open 9.00am–5.00pm, Mon.–Thur.; 9.00am–2.00pm, Fri.

St Patrick's Cathedral

The Library, Abbey Street, Armagh. Tel: 028 37523142 E-mail dean@armagh.anglican.org Web http://www.st.patricks-cathedral.org

Possibly the oldest church in Ulster still in use, St Patrick's is the burial site of Brian Boru, the high king of Ireland who died in battle at Clontarf in 1014. The old cathedral contains the military chapel of the Royal Irish Fusiliers, and the colours of the regiment and those of local militia and volunteer units are on exhibit. The cathedral also displays the colours of French General Humbert's 2nd battalion, 70th Demi-Brigade, captured by the Armagh militia at the battle of Ballinamuck in September 1798.

Open daily, Apr. to Oct., 10.00am-5.00pm; Nov.–Mar., 10.00am–4.00pm. Guided tours, June–Aug.

The Royal Irish Fusiliers Museum

Sovereign's House, Mall East, Armagh, BT61 9DL. Tel: 028 37522911 E-mail Rylirfusiliermus@cs.com Web www.rirfus-museum.freeserve.co.uk

Recently refurbished, the museum holds uniforms, medals and regalia of the regiment, known as the 'Faughs' from their battle cry 'Faugh-a-Ballagh' (Clear the way). Exhibits tell the story of the Royal Irish Fusiliers from its formation in 1793, through the Napoleonic Wars, the Crimean War, the Boer War (where the Faughs relieved the besieged Ladysmith), to extensive service in the First and Second World Wars in which the Fusilers fought at the Somme, Dunkirk, North Africa and in Italy. The regiment amalgamated with the Royal Inniskilling Fusiliers and the Royal Ulster Rifles in 1968 to form the Royal Irish Rangers.

Open 10.00am–12.30pm, 1.00pm–4.00pm, Mon.–Fri. Admission charge.

CARLOW

Carlow Castle
Town centre, Carlow.
The mote was erected by Hugh de Lacy in the 1180s. Later the castle was granted to the earls of Norfolk by the crown. It was captured by James FitzGerald in 1494 and by Silken Thomas in 1535. In 1642 the fortress was occupied by the armies of the Catholic Confederation, only to be retaken by Cromwellian troops eight years later.
Open weekdays.

Carlow Military Museum
Old Church, St Dympna's, Athy Road, Carlow. Tel: 087 2850509 E-mail military.museum@ireland.com
The museum's main focus is on the history of the Irish Defence Forces. Displays feature the uniforms and insignia of the Defence Forces through the years and document their United Nations service in the Congo, Lebanon and Somalia. Other displays focus on the involvement of Carlow people in military service from the Carlow militia to Captain Myles Keogh of the US 7th Cavalry, and up to the First World War.
Open alternate Sundays during spring and summer. Otherwise by appointment. Admission charge.

Carlow Museum
Town Hall, Carlow. Tel: 0503 40730
Collections mainly relating to the social and commercial history of the county.
Open 11.00am–5.00pm., Tue.–Fri.

CAVAN

Cavan County Museum
Virginia Road, Ballyjamesduff, County Cavan. Tel: 049 8544070 Fax: 049 8544332 E-mail ccmuseum@tinet.ie
The county museum contains some material of interest to military historians.
Open 10.00am–5.00pm, Tue.–Sat.; 2.00pm–6.00pm, Sun. (June–Sept. only). Admission charge.

Bunratty Castle

County Clare, Airport road, 8 miles west of Limerick.

Norman castles were built here from 1251 onwards. The Vikings had previously established a fortification here, on a strategic island with a view of river traffic entering and leaving the port of Limerick. The castle was at first the home of the Gaelic MacNamara family but passed through marriage into the hands of the O'Briens of Thomond. The building suffered during the conflicts of the 1600s, when the O'Briens abandoned it. Today it is internationally known for its folk park and medieval banquets.

Open daily, Mon.–Fri., summer, 9.00am–6.30pm; winter, 9.30am–5.30pm.

Carrigaholt Castle

7 miles west of Kilkee, County Clare. (In ruins.)

Built by the McMahons in the fifteenth century, this tower house dominated the Corcabascin peninsula. In 1588 seven ships of the Spanish Armada anchored at Carrigaholt. Soon afterwards, government forces unsuccessfully besieged the castle. In 1589, however, the earl of Thomond captured the castle and killed all its defenders, passing it to his brother's control. Thomond's grandson, Viscount Clare, raised a regiment of horse for James II's armies in the 1680s but, following the victory of the Williamites, the castle and estate were confiscated by the crown.

Accessible, but across fields.

Clare Museum

Arthur's Row, off O'Connell Square, Ennis, County Clare. Tel: 065 682 3382 E-mail claremuseum@eircom.net Web www.clarelibrary.ie/ eolas/claremuseum

The museum holds a number of weapons, medals and memorabilia from the 1798 Rebellion, First and Second World Wars and the War of Independence. These include pike heads from 1798, rifles and revolvers from the 1916–23 period, mines and anti-submarine devices washed ashore during the Second World War and the Africa Star, Italy Star and 1939–45 War medals awarded to Nurse Josephine Canny.

Open all year round. Admission charge.

Craggaunowen
Kilmurry, Sixmilebridge, County Clare. Tel: 061 360788 Fax: 061 361020.
This reconstruction of Celtic village life includes a ring fort.
Open daily, Mar.–Oct. Admission charge.

Dysert O'Dea Castle
Dysert O'Dea, Corofin, County Clare. Tel: 065 6837401
The castle, built in 1480 by Diarmaid O'Dea, was badly damaged by Cromwellian forces in 1651. It is close to the site of the 1318 battle of Dysert O'Dea, where Norman overlord Richard de Clare was defeated and killed by Murtagh O'Brien, king of Thomond, and his allies, the O'Deas. The castle now houses a museum.

Killaloe Heritage Centre
Killaloe, County Clare. Tel: 061 376866
Web www.shannonheritage.com
The centre is devoted to Ireland's Celtic heritage. Killaloe was the birthplace of Brian Boru, king of Munster, and the most successful of the old Irish kings.
Open daily, 10.00am–6.00pm, May–Sept.

Knappogue Castle
Quin, County Clare. Tel: 061 360788
The castle, seat of the MacNamara family from 1467, was occupied by Cromwellian forces as a consequence of Douglas MacNamara's participation in the 1641 Rebellion
Open daily, May–Oct.

CORK

Ballincollig Gunpowder Mills Heritage Centre
Killarney Road, 5 miles from Cork city. Tel: 021 4874430 Fax: 021 4874836
E-mail ballinco@indigo.ie
During the Napoleonic Wars, the British Board of Ordnance bought local mills and turned them into a major arms producing centre, employing 500 local men and boys by the 1880s.
Open daily Apr.–Sept., 10.00am–5.00pm.

Bantry French Armada Centre

East Stables, Bantry House, Bantry, County Cork.

In 1796 a French fleet carrying almost 15,000 troops, among them the United Irish leader Wolfe Tone, almost succeeded in landing on the Cork coast. This centre features audiovisual reconstructions of French naval life and the plans of Tone and the United Irishmen.

Open Apr.–Oct. Admission charge.

Charles Fort

Summer Cove, Kinsale. Tel: 021 4772263 Fax: 021 4774347

One of the largest military forts in Ireland, the construction of this fort commenced in 1677 on the site of a medieval castle, which had itself been occupied by Spanish forces in 1601. The star-shaped Charles Fort saw fighting soon after its construction when it was besieged by the Williamite general, John Churchill, later duke of Marlborough. It was also the scene of fighting during the Irish Civil War.

Open daily in summertime, and at weekends in spring and autumn. Admission charge & regular guided tours.

Cobh Heritage Centre

Cobh, County Cork. Tel: 021 4813591 Fax: 021 4813595 E-mail info@cobhheritage.com

The centre is primarily concerned with the story of Irish emigration but contains some material relating to naval warfare, including the sinking of the *Lusitania.*

Open daily, 10.00am–6.00pm (5.00pm in winter). Admission charge.

Collins Barracks Cork Military Museum

Collins Barracks, Cork. Tel: 021 4514125 and 021 4514126 Fax: 021 4502666

The museum opened in 1985 and was conceived as a tribute to soldiers from the barracks who lost their lives in the line of duty. Its core collection is that of memorabilia associated with Michael Collins, including his personal diary, some personal papers, two of his revolvers and his War of Independence medal. In addition, the museum houses a large photographic collection dedicated to the history of the barracks.

Access is restricted. Write to O/C, Collins Barracks, Cork.

Conna Castle
In the Slane valley, 4 miles west of Tullow.
Built in the 1550s by Sir Thomas Roe FitzGerald, the castle was lost to the earl of Essex after FitzGerald joined the 1599 revolt. In 1645 the castle was captured by Confederate Catholic forces and its garrison killed.

Cork Public Museum
FitzGerald Park, Mardyke, Cork. Tel: 021 4270679 Fax: 021 4270931
E-mail museum@corkcorp.ie
The museum holds an extensive collection relating to the War of Independence period in Cork, with artefacts and memorabilia belonging to Tom Barry, Terence MacSwiney and Thomas MacCurtain. Uniforms, medals and weapons are among the exhibits. A small number of collections relate to the involvement of Cork people in the American Civil War.
Open 11.00am–1.00pm, 2.15pm–5.00pm, Mon.–Fri.; 3.00–5.00pm, Sun. Admission free.

Desmond Castle
Cork Street, Kinsale. Tel: 021 477 4855
Built in 1500, this castle was captured by the Spanish in the winter of 1601, during the battle of Kinsale; it was used to hold captured American sailors during the American Revolution. It is known locally as the 'French Prison' after 54 French prisoners burned to death here in 1747.
Open Apr.–June, 10.00am–6.00pm, Tue.–Sun.; daily June–Oct., 10.00am–6.00pm. Admission charge.

Kinsale Museum
Market Square, Kinsale. Tel: 021 4777930 Web http://homepage.tinet.ie/~kinsalemuseum/index.html
The battle of Kinsale was a decisive turning point in Irish history, bringing to an end a nine-year rebellion which had seen a powerful alliance of Ulster Gaelic chieftains drive the English from that province and spread insurrection throughout Ireland. A Spanish expeditionary force landed in the Kinsale area in September 1601 but was besieged by English forces under Lord Deputy Mountjoy. A large army of Gaelic soldiers led by Hugh O'Neill and Red Hugh O'Donnell marched from Ulster to join forces with the Spanish. Despite early successes, the Irish forces were routed in early 1602 and the Spanish agreed to withdraw. The defeat ended Spain's immediate interest in Ireland

and broke the Ulster lords' resistance, setting the scene for plantation and conquest. The museum contains a major exhibition on this episode. There are also collections relating to the sinking of the *Lusitania* in 1915.
Open 10.00am–5.00pm, Sat.; 2.00pm–5.00pm, Sun.

Mallow Castle
Mallow, County Cork. (In ruins.)
A fortress of the Desmond family, it was granted in 1584 to Sir Thomas Norreys, lord president of Munster. It held out against the Confederates in 1642 but was eventually captured in 1645 and fell into disuse soon after.

West Cork Regional Museum
Western Road, Clonakilty, County Cork.
The museum's main exhibition focuses on the War of Independence in west Cork. Arms and militaria are displayed and there is a special emphasis on the career of Michael Collins.

DERRY/LONDONDERRY

Derry City Walls
Having withstood the famous 105-day siege by Jacobite forces in 1689, Derry is the only remaining completely walled city in Ireland. The walls encircle the old city, a circuit of one mile and are open to the public from dawn till dusk. Admission free.

The Tower Museum
Union Hall Place, Derry City. Tel: 028 71372411
The award-winning museum holds numerous artefacts relating to the siege in 1689, the conflicts between 1912 and 1922 and the impact of both world wars on the area.
Open Sept.–June, 10.00am–5.00pm, Tues.–Sat. & Bank Holidays; July–Aug., 10.00am–5.00pm, Mon.–Sat. Admission charge.

St Columb's Cathedral
London Street, Derry City. Tel: 028 71267313
The cathedral's museum contains artefacts from the siege of Derry. The cathedral itself houses a set of *Ireland's Memorial Records* of World War

One, memorials to local war dead as well as British and United States regimental and naval flags. A mortar ball which contained a Jacobite note demanding Derry's surrender in 1689 is on display in the cathedral.
Open Mon.–Sat., summer 9.00am–5.00pm, winter 9.00am–1.00pm, 2.00pm–4.00pm. Admission donation.

Plantation of Ulster Centre
50 High Street, Draperstown, County Derry. Tel: 028 7962 7800 Fax: 028 7962 7732 E-mail info@theflightoftheearlsexperience.com Web www.theflightoftheearlsexperience.com
This interactive museum and heritage centre explains the military and political background to the Ulster Plantations that followed the Flight of the Earls in 1607.
Open Easter–Sept., 10.00am–5.00pm, Mon.–Sat., 1.00pm–5.00pm, Sun.; Oct.–Easter, 10.00am–4.00pm, Mon.–Fri. Admission charge.

The Workhouse Museum
23 Glendermott Road, Derry City. Tel: 028 71318328
The museum's first floor houses the *Atlantic Memorial* exhibition that details the role the city played during the battle of the Atlantic. The exhibition contains uniforms, paper items, original artefacts and models.
Open Mon.–Thur., Sat., 10.00am–4.00pm. July–Aug. also open Fri. Admission free.

DONEGAL

Doe Castle
2 miles-north east of Creeslough on the coast, by Sheephaven bay.
Built in the 1520s by MacSweeney Doe, head of a branch of the O'Donnell family, the castle was subjected to over twenty sieges before being abandoned in the late 1600s. Sailors from the Spanish Armada were afforded refuge at the castle in 1588. In 1601 Red Hugh O'Donnell seized the castle, as did Confederate Catholics in 1641, the Cromwellians in 1650 and both Jacobites and Williamites during the 1690s.

Donegal Castle
Donegal Town. Tel: 074 9722405 Fax: 074 9722436
Built in the 1400s, this castle became the chief seat of the powerful O'Donnell clan. After the Flight of the Earls, the O'Donnell lands were

granted to the Brooke family, who successfully defended the castle during the 1641 Rebellion and the Jacobite Wars.
Open Mar.–Oct. daily; Nov.–Jan. weekends.

Donegal County Museum
High Road, Letterkenny, County Donegal. Tel: 074 9124613
Exhibits chart the history of the county and include a section on the Emergency.
Open daily. Admission free.

Flight of the Earls Heritage Centre
Rathmullan Harbour, County Donegal. Tel: 074 9158131 Web www.flightoftheearls.com
Based in a fort constructed during the Napoleonic Wars and situated close to where the 'Flight' took place, exhibits explain how in 1607 Hugh O'Neill, earl of Tyrone, along with Rory O'Donnell, earl of Tyrconnell, and Cuchonnacht Maguire, lord of Fermanagh, fled Ireland. The government declared their leaving treasonous and confiscated their lands to make way for the Ulster Plantation.
Open Easter weekend, mid-May–mid-Sept., 10.00am–6.00pm, Mon.–Sat.; 12.00–6.00pm, Sun. Admission charge.

Fort Dunree Military Museum
Dunree, Linsfort, Buncrana, County Donegal. Tel: 074 9361817 E-mail dunree@eircom.net Web www.dunree.pro.ie
Originally built to guard against French naval incursion between 1798 and 1800, by 1900 Fort Dunree was a modern coastal defence fortification. During October 1914 its guns protected the British Grand Fleet while it sheltered in Lough Swilly. In 1938 the fort was handed over to the Irish Defence Forces and was an important part of the defence effort during the Emergency. It continued as a base for military training until the 1980s. The museum uses interactive technology to bring to life the history of the fort.
Open June–Sept., 10.30am–6.00pm, Mon.–Sat.; 1.00pm–6.00pm., Sun.

Greencastle (Northburgh)
East of Greencastle village, on Inishowen shore of Lough Foyle. (In ruins.)
Built by the earl of Ulster, Richard de Burgo, in 1305 to subdue the O'Donnells and O'Neills, the castle was an important strategic post controlling entry to Lough Foyle. In 1316 it was captured by Edward Bruce. Following the murder of William de Burgo in 1333, the de Burgos lost their

power in the region, and the castle passed into the control of the O'Dohertys. However, in 1555 it was almost destroyed during fighting between the O'Dohertys and O'Donnells and, although garrisoned by crown forces into the 1600s, it was eventually abandoned.

Grianan of Aileach

Off Letterkenny–Derry road, Inishowen.

This was an ancient fort and stronghold of the O'Neills of Ulster from the fifth to the twelfth centuries, until its destruction by Murtagh O'Brien of Munster in 1101. Set 800 feet above sea level, the fort provides spectacular views of Lough Foyle and Lough Swilly.

Old Courthouse, Lifford

Tel: 074 9141733 Web www.infowing.ie/seat of power E-mail seatofpower @tinet.ie

Built originally in 1746, the courthouse was the scene of the trial of United Irishman Napper Tandy. Audio-visual displays explain the background to the O'Donnell clan's dominance of Donegal proir to the Flight of the Earls.

Open daily.

DOWN

Down County Museum

The Mall, Downpatrick, County Down BT30 6AH. Tel: 028 44615218 Fax: 028 44615590 E-mail Museum@downdc.gov.uk

The museum is situated in the former Down county gaol, in which the United Irish leader Thomas Russell was imprisoned prior to his public execution in 1803. The muscum holds matcrial relating to the 1798 and 1803 rebellions, including weapons and documents. There are also exhibits on the Ulster and Irish Volunteers from 1912 onwards and substantial collections relating to the two world wars.

Open Mon.–Fri., 10.00am–5.00pm; Sat. & Sun., 1.00pm–5.00pm. Admission free.

Dundrum Castle

Dundrum, County Down.

Founded by John de Courcy in 1177, the castle was seized from him by King John in 1210. The castle was in turn taken by the Maginnis family in the 1300s, who held it until expelled by Lord Mountjoy in 1601. The

Maginnis family retook the castle during the 1641 Rebellion, but it was captured and dismantled by Cromwellian forces in 1652.

Grey Point Fort
The Fort, Helen's Bay, County Down BT19 1LE. Tel: 028 91853621 Web www.ehsni.gov.uk
A coastal artillery site was built at Grey Point on the shores of Belfast Lough between 1904 and 1907, to provide security for Belfast port. Housing 6 in. guns and two saluting guns, it was operational during both world wars and remained manned until 1957. On 3 September 1939 the fort's guns fired the British Army's first shots of the Second World War. With the fort's closure, its weapons were removed. When in 1987 the fort was restored as a historic site, two 6 in. guns were donated by the Irish Defence Forces from coastal defence forts in Cork Harbour.
Open All year round, 10.00am–5.00pm. Admission free.

Green Castle
Seashore Carlingford Lough off A2 Kilkeel–Warrenpoint road. Tel: 028 9054 3037 E-mail sc@doeni.gov.uk
Built in the mid-thirteenth century, the castle commanded the sea link to Carlingford. It was besieged and captured by Edward Bruce in 1316. It was again besieged in 1333–4 and taken by Irish forces in 1343 and 1375. In 1505 it was granted to the earls of Kildare but was destroyed by Cromwellian forces in 1652.
Guided tours available.

Jordan's Castle
Ardglass, County Down.
Built in the 1400s to defend the seaport of Ardglass, this castle withstood a lengthy siege during Tyrone's rebellion.
Open to the public.

North Down Heritage Centre
Town Hall, Bangor, County Down. Tel: 028 270371 Fax: 271370
The centre houses material relating to the social history of the county.
Open daily, 10.30am–4.30pm.

The Somme Heritage Centre

233 Bangor Road, Newtownards, County Down, BT23 7PH Tel: 028 4782 3202 E-mail Sommeassociation@dnet.co.uk Web www.irishsoldier. org

This heritage centre holds over 5000 artefacts dealing with the First World War. Education is at the heart of the Centre's activities, and guided tours and education packs aimed at schoolgoers are available. Elements of the battlefields of the war are reconstructed in a multi-media exhibition, and the political background to pre-war Ireland is illustrated through the use of material from the Irish and Ulster Volunteers. There is a database of Irish fatalities of the Great War for those wishing to trace details of relatives. The Somme Association, which coordinates research into Ireland's part in the First World War, is based at the centre.

Open 10.00am–4.00pm, Mon.–Thur.; 12.00pm–4.00pm, Sat. & Sun.

DUBLIN

Arbour Hill Cemetery

Arbour Hill, Dublin 7.

The 1916 memorial, located in the cemetery at the rear of the church of the Sacred Heart, contains the graves of 14 of the executed leaders of the 1916 Rising. The cemetery also contains the graves of many soldiers who died whilst serving with the British Army in Dublin. The colours of various battalions of the Defence Forces, formed to serve with the United Nations are laid up in the church of the Sacred Heart. The church also contains a number of regimental plaques.

Open daily, 9.00am–5.00pm.

Bank of Ireland

College Green, Dublin 2.

Situated within the bank and open to the public is the former House of Lords of the Irish parliament during the eighteenth century. On facing walls are tapestries commemorating the battle of the Boyne and the siege of Derry. College Green was the site for numerous mobilizations of the Volunteer movement during the 1780s. The cannon, a carronade, situated in the bank's forecourt dates from the period of the Napoleonic Wars.

Open 10.00am–4.00pm, Mon.–Fri.

Christchurch Cathedral, Dublin
Tel: 01 6778099 Web www.cccdub.ie/visitors/visitinfo.html
The cathedral is the burial place of many of the first Anglo-Norman lords of Dublin and site of memorials to Irish dead of the two world wars.
Open 9.45am–5.00pm, Mon.–Fri.; 10.00am–5.00pm, Sat. & Sun. Admission donation.

City Hall
Dame Street, Dublin 2. Tel: 01 6722204 Fax: 01 6722620
E-mail cityhall@dublincity.ie Web www.dublincity.ie
A permanent multi-media exhibition, *The Story of the Capital,* includes many references to the experience of warfare in Dublin from the Viking period onwards. City Hall itself was the scene of fighting during the 1916 Rising, and a plaque commemorates members of the Irish Citizen Army killed there.
Open 10.00am–5.15pm, Mon.–Sat.; 2.00pm–5.00pm, Sun. Admission charge.

Civic Museum
58 South William Street, Dublin 2. Tel: 01 6794260
Exhibits deal with the social, economic and political history of Dublin.
Open 10.00am–6.00pm, Tues.–Sat.; 11.00am–2.00pm, Sun. Admission free.

Croppies' Acre Memorial Garden
Collins Barracks, Dublin 7.
The portion of the esplanade in front of Collins Barracks is called the Croppie's Acre because hundreds of executed rank and file of the 1798 Rebellion are said to be buried there. An official memorial was formally unveiled here in 1998.

Dublin Castle
Dame Street, Dublin 2. Tel: 01 6777129 Fax: 01 6797831
Built originally in the thirteenth century, it functioned as a prison, treasury, courts of law and military fortress but most famously as the seat of English and British administration in Ireland; hence it was subject to numerous sieges and attacks over the centuries. Its Heraldic Museum holds a collection of flags of the eighteenth-century Irish regiments of France.
Open Courtyard, daily, 10.00am–5.00pm. Admission free.

State apartments 10.00am–5.00pm, Mon.–Fri.; 2.00pm–5.00pm, Sat., Sun. and Bank Holidays. Admission charge.

Gaelic Athletic Association Museum

New Cusack Stand, Croke Park, Dublin 3. Tel: 01 8558176 Fax: 01 8558104 E-mail gaamuseum@crokepark Web www.gaa.ie/museum/

This museum holds many sources related to the development of militant nationalism in the early twentieth century as well as from the 1916–21 period. The Croke Park stadium itself was the scene of the November 1920 Bloody Sunday killings.

Open May–Sept., 9.30am–5.00pm, Mon.–Sat.; Oct.–Apr., 10.00am–5.00pm, Mon.–Sat.; 12.00pm–5.00pm, Sun. (restrictions on match days). Admission charge.

Garda Síochána Museum and Archives

The Records Tower, Dublin Castle, D 2. Tel: 01 6719597

Web www.esatclear.ie/~garda/index.html

The museum features exhibits relating to the history of the Garda from 1922 as well as material on policing in Ireland prior to then.

Open 9.00am–5.00pm, Mon.–Fri. Admission free.

Garden of Remembrance

Parnell Square East, Dublin 1. Tel: 01 8743074

This memorial garden was opened in 1966 and is dedicated to those who gave their lives for Irish independence.

Open daily, summer 9.30am–8.00pm; winter 11.00am–4.00pm. Admission free.

General Post Office

O'Connell Street, Dublin 1.

The headquarters of the 1916 rebels, the GPO was almost destroyed by shelling during the Rising; it was reopened in 1928. The 1916 memorial is in the main hall.

Open Mon.–Sat.

Glasnevin Cemetery

Finglas Road, Dublin 11. Tel: 01 8301133 Fax: 01 8301594 E-mail cemetery@indigo.ie

This is the final resting place of many connected to the Irish nationalist and

republican movement, among them Arthur Griffith, Michael Collins, Eamon de Valera, Countess Markievicz, Roger Casement and Kevin Barry. The cemetery's republican plot includes memorials to the republican dead of the Civil War, while the Irish Defence Forces' plot commemorates the Free State Army's dead of the same conflict. There are also memorials to the Connaught Rangers mutineers of 1920, to the Fenians, and to the 'Mountjoy 10' re-interred in 2001.
Open daylight hours. Admission free. Tours Wed. and Fri.

Irish Jewish Museum
3–4 Walworth Road, South Circular Road, Dublin 8. Tel: 01 4531797/ 6760737
The museum holds some material on the involvement of Irish Jews in warfare, such as Robert Briscoe, IRA gunrunner during the War of Independence and later lord mayor of Dublin.
Open May–Sept., 11.00am–3.30pm, Sun., Tue., Thur.; Oct.–Apr., 10.30am–2.30pm, Sun. only. Donations accepted.

Kilmainham Gaol
Inchicore Road, Dublin 8. Tel: 01 4535984 Fax: 01 4532037
Today one of the largest unoccupied gaols in Europe, Kilmainham housed rebel prisoners in 1798, 1803, 1848, 1867, 1916 and 1919–23. Numerous personalities from Irish history such as Robert Emmet, Charles Stewart Parnell, James Connolly and Eamon de Valera were imprisoned here. It was the scene of many executions and dramatic escapes and continued in use until the end of the Civil War. Its museum has a comprehensive exhibition of materials relating to Irish history. Guided tours of the prison are conducted daily, on the hour. The gaol and museum are often extremely busy during the summer months.
Open daily, Apr.–Sept., 9.30am–6.00pm (last admission 4.45pm); Oct.–Mar., 9.30am–5.30pm, Mon.–Sat. (last admission 4.00pm); 10.00am–6.00pm, Sun. (last admission 4.45pm). Tours last one hour – allow extra 30 minutes to see exhibition. Admission charge.

Maritime Institute of Ireland, Dun Laoghaire
The Mariners Church, Haigh Terrace, Dun Laoghaire. Tel: 01 2800969 Web www.mii.connect.ie

Among the items of military interest on display are the Bantry Boat, a 38-ft officers' barge, captured during the failed French landing of 1796, and the Irish merchant ship *Kerlogue* that rescued 168 German sailors in the Bay of Biscay during 1943. The museum also houses a permanent display of models, photographs, documents and uniforms that commemorates the Naval Service.
Closed for renovation as of October 2003.

The National Museum of Ireland, Collins Barracks
Benburb Street, Dublin 7. Tel: 01 6777444 Fax: 01 6777828
Situated in a former military barracks, from 2005 this museum will include a major permanent exhibition dealing with Ireland's military heritage. While other areas of the museum will deal with the military history of Ireland until 1600, the new exhibition will bring the story up to the present day. The social, cultural and economic background to Irish military involvement will be explained. Themes covered will be 'War in Ireland', beginning with the battle of Kinsale in 1601 and ending with the Civil War of 1922–3, and 'Irish soldiers in foreign armies' – the Wild Geese in Austria, France and Spain, and armed forces of many other countries including Britain, the United States of America, Australia and New Zealand. It will tell the story of Irish men and women who served at home and abroad in whatever country and for whatever cause they chose. The final theme is that of the Irish Defence Forces from its origins in 1913 to the present day.
Open 10.00am–5.00pm, Tues.–Sat.; 2.00pm–5.00pm, Sun. Admission free.

The National Museum of Ireland, Kildare Street
Kildare Street, Dublin 2. Tel: 01 6777444 Fax: 01 6766116
Permanent exhibitions on the impact of Viking and Norman settlement contain much of military interest. 'Kings, Lords and Warriors' deals with the wars of the Norman era and includes exhibits such as an early siege gun. Medals and flags conserved from the 19th century include those relating to the Young Irelanders and the Fenians. The museum also contains a permanent exhibition entitled 'The Road to Independence' which features uniforms, weapons, medals and flags from the 1912–23 period. Included among the exhibits are handguns and uniforms that belonged to Patrick Pearse, Countess Markievicz, Ernie O'Malley, Michael Collins and Eamon de Valera.
Open 10.00am–5.00pm, Tues.–Sat.; 2.00pm–5.00pm, Sun. Admission free.

National War Memorial Park

Islandbridge, Dublin 8. Tel: 01 6472498 or 01 6770236
Site of the War Memorial Gardens built as a permanent tribute to the Irish dead of World War One, the gardens now also commemorate Irish fatalities of World War Two. Sunken rose gardens and extensive tree-planting make the site an area of great beauty. Four granite Bookrooms contain the names of the Irish dead of 1914–1918 in *Ireland's Memorial Records*.
Open 8.00am–dusk, Mon.–Fri.; 10.00am–dusk, Sat. & Sun. Access to Bookrooms by arrangement with management. Admission free.

Pearse Museum and St Enda's Park

St Enda's Park, Grange Road, Rathfarnham, Dublin 16. Tel: 01 4934208 Fax: 01 4936120
Situated in the building that housed the school run by the 1916 rebel leader, the museum features an audiovisual presentation 'This Man Kept a School' along with attractive gardens and nature walks.
Open daily, May–Aug., 10.00am–8.00pm; Sept.–Oct., 10.00am–7.00pm; Nov.–Mar., 10.00am–4.30pm. Admission free.

Royal Hospital Kilmainham

Military Road, Kilmainham, Dublin 8. Tel: 01 6129900
Built in 1683 as a hospital for invalided soliders and modelled on Les Invalides in Paris, this magnificent building today houses the Museum of Modern Art.

FERMANAGH

Enniskillen Castle

Castle Barracks, Enniskillen, County Fermanagh. Tel: 028 66325000 Fax: 028 66327342 E-mail castle@fermanagh.gov.uk Web www.enniskillencastle.co.uk
The castle was built in the 1400s as a stronghold of local Gaelic chieftains the Maguires, whose rule was interrupted periodically by attacks from the neighbouring O'Neills and O'Donnells. In the 1600s English forces took the castle and the plantation town of Enniskillen took its name from the building. Later it became the headquarters of the Royal Inniskilling Fusiliers. Today Enniskillen Castle comprises the castle keep and an array of nine-

teenth-century barracks buildings. Fermanagh County Museum is located in the latter while the castle keep is home to the Inniskillings Museum.
Open Mon.–Fri.; Sun., July and August only. Admission charge.

Fermanagh County Museum

Enniskillen Castle, County Fermanagh. Tel: 028 663 25000 Fax: 028 663 27342

The museum's colourful exhibits and audio-visual programmes relate to the history, wildlife and landscape of Fermanagh.

Open all year round, Mon.–Sat.; July and Aug., Sun. only.

Old Crom Castle.

Crom, west of Newtownbutler.

Built only in 1611, the castle withstood two Jacobite sieges in 1689.

Open to the public.

The Inniskilling Museum

Enniskillen Castle, Castle Barracks, Enniskillen, County Fermanagh BT74 7HL. Tel: 028 6632 3142 Fax: 028 6632 0359

The museum's collections trace the history of the Royal Inniskilling Fusiliers and the 5th Royal Inniskilling Dragoon Guards from their formation in 1688–9. Uniforms, medals, weapons and photographs and regimental memorabilia are open for display. Eight Victoria Crosses, awarded to the regiment during World War One, and the bugle which sounded the advance of the 36th (Ulster) Division on the first day of the battle of the Somme, are also held in the museum. War diaries and archival material are available for research purposes and can be seen by appointment.

Open all year round: Mon. 2.00pm–5.00pm, Tues.–Fri. 10.00am–5.00pm; and additionally, in May–Sept., Sat. and Sun. 2.00pm–5.00pm. Admission charge.

Tully Castle

West shore of Lower Lough Erne, on A46 Enniskillen–Belleek Road. Tel: 028 9054 3037 E-mail sc@doeni.gov.uk

Built during the Ulster plantation by the Hume family, it was captured and burned by the Maguires during the rebellion of 1641 and its inhabitants massacred.

Open to the public.

Athenry Castle

Athenry, County Galway. Tel: 091 844797 Fax: 091 845796 E-mail athenrycastle@ealga.ie

A Norman fortification built by Meiler de Bermingham from 1250 onwards, its walls were completed by 1316. It was captured and destroyed by Red Hugh O'Donnell in 1596. It now houses an audiovisual exhibition.

Open Apr.–Oct., 10.00am–5.00pm, Tues.–Sun. (June–mid Sept., open Mon.). Admission charge.

Aughnanure Castle

Oughterard, County Galway. Tel: 091 552214 Fax: 091 557244

This castle was built by the O'Flahertys in 1500 on what is virtually a rocky island close to Lough Corrib.

Open May–mid June, 9.30am–6.00pm, Sat. and Sun.; daily, mid June–Sept., 9.30am–6.00pm; Oct., 9.30am–6.00pm, Sat. and Sun. Admission charge.

Battle of Aughrim Interpretative Centre

Aughrim, Ballinasloe, County Galway. Tel: 09096 73939

The centre commemorates the key Williamite victory of July 1691, which saw 45,000 soldiers from across Europe join in battle at this site. St Ruth, the Jacobite commander, made his stand here after retreating from Athlone, but was outflanked; he died early in the battle; some 7,000 Jacobite troops were killed, many as they fled, and the back of Jacobite resistance in Ireland was broken. Exhibits explain the background to the war in England's Glorious Revolution (1688), and its aftermath with the departure of the Wild Geese from Ireland.

Open June–Sept., guided tours available – battlefield signposted. Admission charge.

Fiddaun Castle

5 miles south west of Gort, County Galway.

Built during the 1500s for the O'Shaughnessy family, it was forfeited to the crown in 1697 because of the participation of Sir William O'Shaughnessy in the Jacobite armies. He fled to France and became a mareschal de camp in 1734.

Military Museum, Dún Ui Mhaoiliosa

Renmore Barracks, Galway. Tel: 091 701054, 087 9083105 For visits 091 751156 E-mail pssrenmore@eircom.net

Formerly the depot of the Connaught Rangers, Renmore has been an Irish Army base since 1922. Several exhibits commemorate the Connaught Rangers with uniforms, weapons and a regimental drum on display. The War of Independence and Civil War displays include weapons landed from the *Asgard* in 1914, and guns belonging to Dan Breen, Michael Collins and the Countess Markievicz. There is also a motorcycle belonging to IRA leader Liam Mellows. Among the items featured from the Emergency period is a parachute used by downed German airmen in Galway. Finally the various peacekeeping missions of the Defence Forces are featured, most poignantly by weapons from the 1960 Niemba ambush in the Congo in which nine Irish soldiers were killed.

Visits by appointment *only* – call a week in advance if possible.

Pearse Cottage

Ros Muc, off R340 road. Tel: 091 574292.

The summer residence of the 1916 leader, destroyed during the War of Independence, it now features an exhibition on his life.

Open Easter weekend, 10.00am–5.00pm; daily, June–Sept., 10.00am–6.00pm. Admission charge.

Oranmore Castle

The stronghold of the Anglo-Norman Clanricarde family, it was surrendered to Cromwellian forces in 1651, the Clanricardes having joined the 1641 Rebellion.

Wild Geese Heritage Museum and Library

Auvergne Lodge, Dominic Street, Portumna, County Galway. Tel: 09496 41138 E-mail wildgeese@indigo.ie Web http://indigo.ie/~wildgees/

This museum, dedicated to the Irish soldiers who fled into foreign service after 1691, aims to become an international research centre on the subject.

KERRY

Carrigafoyle Castle

2 miles north of Ballylongford. (In ruins.)

Built in the late 1400s by the O'Connors of Kerry, the castle saw several bloody sieges. In 1580 it was held for the earl of Desmond by a combined force of Irish, Italian and Spanish troops. Then Lord Justice Sir William Pelham besieged and captured the building and hanged all its defenders.

Kerry County Museum
Thomas Ashe Memorial Hall, Tralee. Tel: 066 7127777 E-mail info@kerrymuseum.ie
The museum holds a number of items relating to the War of Independence including Irish Volunteers' minute books and activists' diaries.
Open daily June–Aug., 9.30am–5.30pm; for other times, see www.kerrymuseum.ie.

Michael J. Quill Visitor Centre
Kilgarvan, County Kerry. Tel: 064 85511
Dedicated to Quill, a local veteran of the War of Independence and Civil War, the centre houses some exhibits on the revolutionary period.
Open daily, Apr.–Sept. Admission free.

Ross Castle
Killarney, County Kerry. Tel: 064 35851/2
Built in the late fifteenth century by the O'Donoghue Ross chieftains, the castle is considered typical of Irish chieftains' strongholds in that period.
Open daily Apr.–Oct., 10.00am–5.30pm. Admission charge.

KILDARE

Athy Heritage Centre
Town Hall, Athy, County Kildare. Tel: 05986 33075 Fax: 05986 33076 E-mail athyheritage@eircom.net
Important collections devoted to the rich military history of this county, such as the 1798 Rebellion and especially the First World War, are housed at the centre.
Open 10.00am–6.00pm, Mon.–Sat.; 2.00pm–6.00pm, Sun. Admission charge.

Leixlip Castle
Built by the Anglo-Norman de Hereford family in 1171, the castle was besieged by Edward Bruce in 1317. It then became the stronghold of the powerful

Kildare FitzGeralds, one of the pre-eminent families of medieval Ireland, until it was seized following the rebellion of 'Silken Thomas' FitzGerald in 1534.

Maynooth Castle

Maynooth, County Kildare. Tel: 01 6286744 Fax: 01 6286848
E-mail maynoothcastle@duchas.ie
This great stone castle, built around 1200, was the principal stronghold of the Kildare FitzGeralds, one of Ireland's most powerful families of the late Middle Ages. In 1316 King Edward II raised John fitz Thomas FitzGerald to the earldom of Kildare for his 'good-service' in leading an army against Edward Bruce. The FitzGeralds were a major force in Ireland during the fifteenth and sixteenth centuries, and Maynooth Castle was lavishly furnished and expanded. However, in 1534, 'Silken Thomas' FitzGerald rebelled against the crown. His army besieged Dublin, but a strong English force pushed him back into Kildare. His castle was captured by Henry VIII's lord deputy in Ireland, Sir William Skeffington, in 1535 after a siege involving one of the first uses of siege guns in Ireland. Despite the garrison's surrender, many were put to the sword. Maynooth Castle again saw fighting during the 1641 Rebellion and was dismantled after capture by the forces of Eoghan Roe O'Neill in 1647. Exhibition and guided tours available.
Open June–Oct., 10.00am–6.00pm, Mon.–Fri.; 1.00pm–6.00pm, Sat., Sun. & Bank Holidays; Oct., 1.00pm–5.00pm, Sun. Admission charge.

KILKENNY

Kilkenny Castle

Kilkenny City. Tel: 056 7721450 Fax: 056 7763488
This is a twelfth-century castle which for many years was the seat of the Butler family, the dukes of Ormonde. Kilkenny Castle was at the centre of power-struggles in medieval Ireland, with several parliaments being held there. During the Civil War, anti-Treaty forces occupied it briefly.
Open daily, Apr.–May, 10.30am–5.00pm; June–Aug., 9.30am–5.00pm; Oct.–Mar., 10.30am–12.45pm, 2.00pm–5.00pm. Admission charge. Guided tour only.

Nore View Folk Museum

Bennetsbridge, Kilkenny. Tel: 056 7727749
This folk museum includes exhibits relating to the struggle for independence, 1916-23.

LAOIS

Ballaghmore Castle
Mountrath, County Laois. Tel: 0505 21453
Built by the local Gaelic overlord, MacGiollaphádraig, in 1480, the castle was partially destroyed by Cromwellian forces in 1647.

Dunamase Castle
3 miles west of Stradbally.
Built in the 1200s by the Anglo-Normans, it fell to the O'Mores during the fourteenth century. It was taken from them by Sir Charles Coote in 1641 but retaken by Eoghan Roe O'Neill in 1646. The castle was dismantled after being captured by Cromwellian forces in 1650.

Lea Castle
2 miles west of Portarlington.
Built in the 1200s and owned by Sir William Marshall, the castle was burned in 1285 by the O'Connors, in 1307 by the O'Mores and in 1315 by Edward Bruce. It passed through the ownership of several warring families before it was finally destroyed by Cromwellian forces in 1650.

LEITRIM

Parkes Castle
Fivemile Bourne. Tel: 071 9164149
This was the stronghold of the O'Rourkes, local overlords during the Middle Ages. Sir Brian O'Rourke was executed at Tyburn, London, in 1591.
Open daily, mid Mar.–end Oct., 10.00am–6.00pm. Admission charge.

LIMERICK

Adare Castle
Adare village, County Limerick. (In ruins.)
Built in the early 1200s, the castle was for 300 years a stronghold of the Kildare FitzGeralds. Following the final suppression of the rebellion of

Silken Thomas in 1535, it was granted to the earl of Desmond but was lost to English troops in 1578. There were further sieges in 1579, 1581 and 1600. It was finally destroyed by English troops in 1657.

Carrigogunnell Castle
2 miles north west of Mungret village. (In ruins.)
This 13th-century castle was the property of the O'Briens of Thomond, but in 1536 it was captured by government forces under Lord Deputy Grey, who massacred its garrison. The castle was confiscated from the O'Briens during the Cromwellian forfeitures. In 1691 it was mined and blown up by Williamite troops after its Jacobite defenders had surrendered.

De Valera Museum
Bruree schoolhouse, Bruree, County Limerick. Tel: 063 90900
The National School attended by de Valera is now a museum dedicated to his life.
Open 10.00am–5.00pm, Mon.–Fri.; 2.00pm–5.00pm, Sat. & Sun.

Foynes Flying Boat Museum
Foynes, County Limerick. Tel: 069 65416
During the 1930s and 1940s Foynes was a hub for air travel between the United States and Europe. During the Emergency, key radio and weather surveillance was carried out here. The museum features an exhibition on the war years.
Open daily, Apr.–31 Oct., 10.00am–6.00pm.

King John's Castle
Kings Island, Limerick City. Tel: 061 360788 Fax: 061 361020
Built between 1200 and 1210, the castle was captured by Edward Bruce's forces in 1316, the O'Briens and MacNamaras in 1369, Confederate Catholics in 1642 and Cromwell's army in 1651. It withstood the Williamite army in 1690 but was captured by it a year later.
Open daily, Apr.–Oct., 9.30am–5.30pm; Nov.–Mar., 10.30am–4.30pm. Admission charge.

Limerick City Museum – Jim Kemmy Municipal Museum
Casle Lane, Nicholas Street, Limerick City. Tel: 061 417826 E-mail **lwalsh@limerickcity.ie**

Exhibits of military interest include those on the sieges of the city in the 1640s and 1690s; the history of the Royal Munster Fusiliers during the Boer and First World Wars; and local experience of the turbulent 1916–23 period. There is an extensive collection relating to the stand-off between pro- and anti-Treaty forces in the city during July 1922.
Open 10.00am–5.00pm, Tues.–Sat. Admission free.

LONGFORD

Ballinamuck Battle Heritage Centre
Ballinamuck, County Longford. Tel: 043 24848
The centre commemorates the final battle of the 1798 Rebellion. In September 1798 French troops under General Humbert, having scored successes in the west, eventually surrendered to a British force under General Cornwallis. Honourable terms were offered to the French, but their Irish allies were scattered with great losses. The battlefield itself is signposted, with a walking trail available. There is also a 1798 Garden of Remembrance in the town.
Open 10.00am–6.00pm. Admission charge.

Longford County Museum
Main Street, Longford.
The museum contains some material relating to the career of General Sean Mac Eoin, the leading IRA figure in the Midlands and later chief of staff of the Irish Army.
Open summer months.

Longford Museum and Heritage Centre
Lower Main Street, Longford.
As well as information on the career of Sean Mac Eoin, the centre also holds material relating to the relationship between Michael Collins and Kitty Kiernan.
Open June–Sept.

Military Barracks
Church Street, Longford.
Built on the site of the original castle and market house and converted to a barracks in the eighteenth century. Renamed the Sean Connolly Barracks in 1922.

Boyne Valley site

Oldbridge estate. On the south bank of the river Boyne, via the approach from Slane or Drogheda by Donore village or from N51 across Obelisk Bridge.
Tel: 041 9884343 Fax: 041 988 4323 E-mail battleoftheboyne@ealga.ie

The site of the famous engagement in July 1690, when King James II and King William III led over 60,000 men into battle against each other. James' army hoped to cut off the Williamite advance towards Dublin but instead were outflanked and forced to retreat, without fighting a major engagement. Hence losses on both sides were relatively light, with about 1,000 Jacobites and 500 Williamites killed. The presence of both James and William at the battle and its subsequent adoption as the central festival of the Orange Order have made it possibly the best known military encounter in Irish history. However, it was less strategically important than the Williamite victory at Aughrim a year later. The area is under development as an historical site.

Guided tour – outdoors.

Castleroche

Built by the Anglo-Norman de Verdun family, this castle was one of the frontier outposts of the English Pale. It is close to the site of the battle of Faughart (nr. Dundalk) in 1318, which occasioned the death of Edward Bruce. The castle itself was burnt down in 1332.

Drogheda Heritage Centre

Mary Street, Drogheda.

This centre houses several interactive social history displays.

Dundalk County Museum

Jocelyn Street, Dundalk, County Louth. Tel: 042 9327056 Fax: 042 9327058
E-mail dlkmuseum1@eircom.net

The museum exhibits outline the story of Louth from ancient times to the present day.

Open 10.30am–5.30pm, Tues.–Sat.; 2.00pm–6.00pm, Sun.

Millmount Museum

Millmount, Drogheda, County Louth. Tel: 041 9833097 Fax: 041 9841599
E-mail info@millmount.net

This museum is located in the former officers' quarters of a barracks. Historically, Millmount was the site of a Norman fortification and was the scene of fighting during Cromwell's siege of the town in 1649. The museum holds weapons and memorabilia relating to local involvement in the Williamite Wars, the 1798 Rebellion, the 1867 Fenian Rebellion, the 1916-23 period and the First and Second World Wars. Of particular interest are exhibits dealing with the bloody capture of the town by Cromwell and the battle of the Boyne. There is now a fully restored Martello tower dating from the Napoleonic Wars open to the public. The tower itself was the scene of fighting in 1922 during the Civil War.
Open daily. Admission charge.

MAYO

Clew Bay Heritage Centre
The Quay, Westport, County Mayo. Tel: 098 26852
E-mail westportheritage@ eircom.net
The centre's exhibitions include a section on the War of Independence and Civil War, and a display on the life of Major John MacBride, an officer in the Boer Irish Brigade during the Boer War, who was later executed for his part in the 1916 Rising. The centre also holds a small collection of papers relating to the Westport battalion of the IRA during the War of Independence.

Davitt Museum
Straide, Foxford, County Mayo. Tel: 094 9031022. E-mail davittmuseum@ eircom.net Web http://www.museumsofmayo.com/davitt.htm
The museum commemorates the life of Fenian and Land League leader, Michael Davitt, a key figure during the Land War of the 1880s.
Open daily, 10.00am–6.00pm.

Granuaile Centre
Off main street, Louisburgh, County Mayo. Tel: 098 66195
Displays and an audio-visual presentation tell the story of Grace O'Malley, the legendary 'pirate queen', who dominated this part of the west coast during the late 1500s. Her fleet defeated English forces deployed to subdue her in 1574 and 1579. In 1588 she captured ships belonging to the Spanish Armada and massacred their crews, a service for which Queen Elizabeth received her in state.
Open June–mid Sept.

Rockfleet Castle
5 miles west of Newport, on an inlet of Clew Bay. (In ruins.)
From 1566, Rockfleet was the stronghold of Grace O'Malley, and the base from which her fleet controlled the west coast.

MEATH

Boyne Valley site
Oldbridge estate. On the south bank of the river Boyne, approach from Slane or Drogheda by Donore village or from N51 across Obelisk Bridge. Tel: 041 9884343 Fax: 041 988 4323 E-mail battleoftheboyne@ealga.ie
This is the site of the famous engagement in July 1690, when King James II and King William III led over 60,000 men into battle against each other. See also entry for County Louth.

Donore Castle
8 miles south west of Trim.
Built during the 1400s as part of the English Pale defences, the castle was the scene of the massacre by Cromwellian troops of over forty inhabitants, including the family of its owner, James MacGeoghegan, in 1650.

Ledwidge Museum
Jeanville, Slane, County Meath Tel: 041 9824544
This is the former home of the poet Francis Ledwidge, a member of the Irish Volunteers who joined the Royal Inniskilling Fusiliers in 1914, saw service initially with the 10th (Irish) Division at Gallipoli and was later killed while serving with the 16th (Irish) Division near Ypres, Belgium in 1917.
Open daily, 10.00am–1.00pm, 2.00pm–6.00pm. Admission charge.

Trim Castle
Trim, County Meath. Tel: 046 9438619 Fax: 046 9438618.
The largest Anglo-Norman fortress in Ireland, constructed over a period of thirty years after 1172 by Hugh de Lacy and his son Walter to curb the expansionist policies of rival lord Richard de Clare (Strongbow). The castle had to be rebuilt after an attack by Roderick of Connaught in 1174.
Open daily, Easter–Oct. Guided tours. Admission charge.

(above)
1 Standards of the regiments of Bulkeley, Roscommon, Dillon, Berwick and Clare (18th century).

2 Capture of Bourbon 1810 (Réunion, Indian Ocean), by the 86th Regiment, later the Royal Irish Rifles, renamed Royal Ulster Rifles in 1921.

3 A Royal Irish Rifles ration party resting while moving forward through communications trenches, 1 July 1916.

4 36th (Ulster) Division sentry observing through a box periscope near Essigny on 7 February 1918.

5 Arthur Griffith and Michael Collins with Guard of Honour at Sean Mac Eoin's wedding, June 1922.

6 British forces in Dublin during the War of Independence; two Peerless armoured cars can be seen in the background.

7 Part of the 800-man unit of the National Army marching into Portobello Barracks (17 May 1922) which was being vacated by the British Army as part of the handover agreed in the Anglo-Irish Treaty.

8 The Mole at Dunkirk 1100 hours, 1 June 1940. Having fought a rearguard action, men of the 2nd Battalion, Royal Ulster Rifles await evacuation to England.

9 Members of the 33rd Infantry Battalion of the Irish Defence Forces under instruction in the Congo on the Carl Gustaf 9mm sub machine-gun.

10 Irish troops peacekeeping in South Lebanon

11 The Ulster Crossing on the river Imjin in Korea, 1951. This section of the 38th Parallel was taken and held by the Royal Ulster Rifles during the Korean war.

12 Honours are rendered at the memorial, Camp Shamrock, HQ of the Irish Battalion in UNIFIL, South Lebanon.

Trim Visitors Centre

Old Town Hall, Castle Street, Trim, County Meath. Tel: 046 377227
Exhibits tell the story of the Norman presence in the county.
Open 9.00am–5.00pm, Mon.–Thur; 9.00am–2.00pm, Fri.

MONAGHAN

Monaghan County Museum

1–2 Hill Street, Monaghan. Tel: 047-82928 Fax: 047 71189 E-mail moncomuseum@tinet.ie
The museum contains numerous collections relevant to military history, especially as it impacted on Monaghan. Exhibits deal with the battle of Clontibret (1595), the growth of the Volunteer movement in the 1780s, the yeomanry and rebels of 1798, and the War of Independence and the Civil War.
Open 10.00am–5.00pm, Tues.–Sat. Admission free.

OFFALY

Leap Castle

Leap, County Offaly.
A fortress of the O'Carroll family, the castle survived attacks by the FitzGeralds in 1516 and the earl of Sussex in 1557. After the plantation years, it passed into the ownership of the Darby family. However, it was destroyed in 1922 during the Civil War.
Open to the public.

ROSCOMMON

Ballintober Castle

Village, 11 miles north west of Roscommon.
Built in the 1290s, it was taken over in the mid-1300s by the O'Connors, who made it their chief seat until 1652. In 1598 they were forced to submit to Red Hugh O'Donnell when he attacked the castle with cannon. The O'Connors joined the 1641 Rebellion and, as a result, the castle was confiscated in 1652.

King House

Main Street, Boyle, County Roscommon Tel: 071 9663242 Fax: 071 9663243 E-mail kinghouseboyle@hotmail.com

From 1788 King House was the headquarters of the Roscommon militia; from 1881 the 4th (Militia) Battalion of the Connaught Rangers, was located here. A permanent exhibition traces the history of the Connaught Rangers, focusing on recruitment, living conditions and the regiment's campaigns, including the mutiny in India in July 1920.

Open daily, May–Oct., 10.00am–6.00pm; weekends, Oct.–May, 10.00am–6.00pm.

Roscommon Castle

Roscommon Town. (In ruins.)

Built originally by Robert de Ufford in 1269 as part of an attempt by the Anglo-Normans to establish control west of the Shannon, the castle was partially destroyed by Hugh O'Connor in 1272 and again in 1277. Despite new fortifications, the castle was again stormed by the local lord, Donogh O'Kelly, in 1308. It was captured by government forces in 1569 and granted to Sir Nicholas Malby, governor of Connaught. From 1645 to 1652 it was occupied by Confederate Catholics, and following its capture by Cromwellian troops, it was dismantled.

Roscommon County Museum

John Harrison Memorial Hall, The Square, Roscommon. Tel: 09066 25613

The museum's exhibits deal with the social history of the county.

SLIGO

Ballinafad Castle

6 miles north west of Boyle.

Built in 1590 as a military post to defend pass through the Curlew mountains, in 1642 it was captured by rebels after a short siege.

Ballymote Castle

Ballymote, County Sligo. (In ruins.)

Built after 1300, Ballymote was one of the strongest Norman fortifications in Connaught. In 1317 the castle was captured by the O'Connors and during the following 200 years, possession passed between them and the MacDonaghs.

In 1584 it was garrisoned by English troops, who remained until the arrival of Red Hugh O'Donnell in 1598. It was at Ballymote that O'Donnell assembled his forces for the march to Kinsale in 1601. The castle was captured by Cromwellian forces in 1652 and demolished by Williamite troops in 1690.

Sligo County Museum
Heritage Centre, Stephen Street, Sligo. Tel: 071 9143728
This museum houses artefacts and exhibits of local interest.

TIPPERARY

Cahir Castle
Castle Street, Cahir, County Tipperary. Tel: 052 41011 Fax: 052 42324
A Norman fortification and stronghold of the Butler family; in 1599 the earl of Essex took the castle following a three-day siege, and in 1650 it surrendered to Cromwell's forces. It was used as a military barracks during the Civil War.
Open daily, 9.30am–5.00pm. Guided tours available. Admission charge.

Nenagh Castle
Nenagh, County Tipperary.
Built in 1200 by Theobald Walter, the founder of the Butler dynasty, the castle was captured by the O'Briens during the 1400s but was retaken by the Butlers in 1533. It was finally destroyed by the Williamites following its capture by General Ginkel in 1690.

Tipperary South Riding Museum
The Borstal, Emmet Street, Clonmel, County Tipperary. Tel: 052 34551
E-mail pholland@southtippcoco
Exhibits tell the story of Tipperary's land and its people from the Stone Age to the present day, including the impact of war and conflict on the county, with material on the locally recruited Royal Irish Regiment, the War of Independence and the Civil War.
Open 10.00am–1.00pm, 2.00pm–5.00pm, Tue.–Sat.

The Rock of Cashel
Cashel, County Tipperary. Tel: 062 61437
A fort was built here in the fourth century and the site became the seat of kings and bishops for nearly 900 years. For a long period the residence of

the kings of Munster, the greatest Irish high king, Brian Ború, was crowned king of Munster here in 977. In the twelfth century a chapel was added to the site. In 1647 a Cromwellian force sacked and burned part of the chapel.
Open daily.

1848 Warhouse
Ballingarry, County Tipperary. Tel: 087 9089972
The house was the scene of the abortive Young Ireland rising of 1848. An exhibition explains the political background to the rising and the story of the Young Irelanders.
Open summer 2.30pm–5.30pm, Wed.–Sun.; winter 2.00pm–4.00pm, Sat. & Sun. only. Admission charge: telephone for details.

TYRONE

Benburb Castle
South of the village main street. (In ruins.)
Built between 1611 and 1614, the castle was captured in October 1641 by Phelim O'Neill, who had all its inhabitants put to death. In 1646 Eoghan Roe O'Neill gathered his forces here before he successfully confronted the English at Benburb.

Grant Ancestral Home
Ballygawley, County Tyrone (off A4 to Dungannon). Tel: 028 2527133
Home of the great-grandfather of Ulysses S. Grant, commander of Union armies during the American Civil War and twice president of the United States. Exhibits tell the Grant family story.
Open Mar.–May & Oct., 10.30am–4.30pm, Mon.–Fri.; June–Sept., 10.00am–6.30pm, Mon.–Sat., 2.00pm–6.00pm, Sun. Admission charge.

Ulster American Folk Park
Castletown, Omagh, County Tyrone. Tel: 028 243292 Web http://www.folkpark.com
The park tells the story of Ulster emigration to the Americas in the eighteenth century. Many Ulster emigrants were involved centrally in the conflicts between Britain, France and Spain in the new world, warfare with Native Americans and in the American Revolution.

Open Apr.–Sept., 10.30am–4.30pm, Mon.–Sat., 11.00am–5.00pm, Sun.; Oct.–Mar., 10.30am–3.30pm, Mon.–Fri. Admission charge.

Ulster History Park
Cullion, Lislap, Omagh, County Tyrone. Tel: 028 81648188. E-mail uhp@omagh.gov.uk
This Omagh-based park details the history of Ulster until the seventeenth century.

WATERFORD

Dungarvan Castle
Castle Street, Dungarvan, County Waterford. Tel: 058 48144
This twelfth-century castle incorporates a restored eighteenth-century barracks featuring exhibition and visitor facilities.
Open for guided tours. June–Sept.

Dungarvan Museum
Old Town Hall, St Augustine Street, Dungarvan, County Waterford. Tel: 058 45960 Web www.dungarvanmuseum.org
This museum holds important collections of material relating to local involvement in the First and Second World Wars, the War of Independence, the Civil War and the Emergency. Exhibits also include artefacts dating from the 1798 Rebellion and the Boer War.
Open 10.00am–1.00pm, 2.00pm–4.45pm, Mon.–Sat. Admission free.

Lismore Castle
Built in 1185 by Prince John, the castle was owned for a period by Sir Walter Raleigh. In 1645 it was sacked by Catholic rebel forces. Following his defeat at the battle of the Boyne, King James II stayed here.

Reginald's Tower, Waterford
The Quay, Waterford. Tel: 051 304220
A thirteenth-century tower, originally part of the town defences, it was later used as a prison and military store.

Waterford City Walls
Waterford City Tourist Services, Waterford. Tel: 051 873711
These fortifications date from the Viking and Anglo-Norman period, and are second only to Derry's city walls with six towers still standing. Walking tours available.

WESTMEATH

Athlone Castle
Athlone, County Westmeath. Tel: 09064 72107/92912
A fort stood here from 1129, eventually becoming a Norman castle. For over a week during June 1691, a force of 18,000 Williamite troops under General Ginkel fought to capture the town defended by 23,000 Jacobite soldiers under St Ruth. The castle sustained what was probably the heaviest bombardment in Irish history, with over 12,000 cannon balls and 600 bombs fired at its walls. The story of this siege is illustrated by an exhibition at the castle.
Open daily, May–Sept., and for groups by arrangement.

Columb Barracks and Military Museum
Mullingar, County Westmeath.
While this small museum holds collections relating to the Civil War and World Wars One and Two, a special emphasis is placed on the War of Independence. Access by appointment only. Apply to Officer Commanding.

Tyrrellspass Castle and Museum
Tyrrellspass, County Westmeath. Tel: 044 23105
The castle was built by the Tyrrells, Anglo-Norman lords and cousins of William the Conqueror, *c.*1411.

WEXFORD

Ballyhack Castle
Ballyhack, County Wexford. Tel: 051 389468
Built in 1450 by the Knights Hospitallers, the castle occupies a commanding position overlooking the Waterford estuary.
Visitors are advised to phone in advance.
Admission charge.

Duncannon Fort
Duncannon, County Wexford. Tel: 051 389454
Built in 1588 in expectation of an attack by the Spanish Armada, there was previously a Celtic fort and a Norman castle on the site. Restoration in progress at time of publication.

Enniscorthy Castle and County Wexford Historical and Folk Museum
Enniscorthy, County Wexford. Tel: 054 35926
The castle was built by the Anglo-Norman Prendergast family during the thirteenth century and was owned at one stage by the Elizabethan poet, Edmund Spenser. It was besieged by Cromwellian forces in 1649 and used as a prison during the 1798 Rebellion. The museum contains collections relating to the 1798 Rebellion and the 1916–23 period.
Open daily, Mar.–Sept.; Oct.–Feb. on Sun. only. Admission charge.

Ferns Castle
Ferns, County Wexford. Tel: 056 7724623
The building dates from the 1220s. It was captured by the O'Tooles in 1331 but recovered shortly afterwards and held thereafter by the bishop of Ferns. In the 1370s it was again captured, this time by the MacMurroughs, who lost it to Lord Grey in 1536. The fortress was demolished by Cromwellian soldiers in 1649.
Open daily, mid-June–mid-Sept., 9.30am–6.30pm.

National 1798 Visitor Centre
Enniscorthy, County Wexford. Tel: 054 37596 Fax: 054 37198 E-mail 98com@iol.ie Web www.1798centre.com
Interactive displays explain the political and social background to the rebellion of 1798. Audio-visual presentations bring alive the reality of the bloody warfare that saw eleven major battles take place in Wexford in just four weeks, with 20,000 fatalities. Artefacts and weapons from the period are on permanent display in the museum. School groups are particularly welcome.
Open 9.30am–5.00pm, Mon.–Sat.; 11.00am–5.00pm, Sun. Admission charge.

WICKLOW

Dwyer Cottage
Derrynamuck, Knockanarrigan. Tel: 0404 45325/52

In the aftermath of the defeat of the 1798 Rebellion, United Irishman Michael Dwyer began a three-year guerrilla campaign in the Wicklow Mountains. Surrounded by British troops, he fled this cottage in 1799; today it houses an exhibition on the period.

Open daily, mid-June–mid-Sept., 1.00pm–6.00pm. Admission free.

Wicklow Gaol

Kilmantin Hill, Wicklow town. Tel: 0404 61599 Fax: 0404 61612

Constructed in 1702, this building housed prisoners following the rebellion of 1798. An exhibition covers the gaol's long history, including the impact of the rebellion on Irish society.

Libraries and institutions

LIBRARIES

Frequently the local public library is the best place to start research in the field of military history. Almost all libraries have collections of local newspapers, which will often contain references to the participation of individuals in conflict as well as reports of casualties. These libraries will also hold locally produced journals, magazines, and souvenir booklets that contain information on military history. Some of these may be unavailable elsewhere. To further one's research it is usually necessary to visit either the National Library or a private or specialist library, so it is useful to ascertain opening hours and rules of access.

Allen Library
Edmund Rice House, North Richmond Street, Dublin 1. Tel: 01 8551077 Fax: 01 855 5243 E-mail allenlib@connect.ie Web www.allenlibrary.com
This library houses a large collection of books and journals relating to Irish history, especially the struggle for independence.
Open 10.00am–4.00pm, Mon.–Fri. by appointment.

Belfast Central Library
Royal Avenue, Belfast BT1 1EA. Tel: 028 90243233 E-mail info@libraries.belfast-elb.gob.uk
The library's Belfast, Ulster and Irish Studies department has a complete set of *Ireland's Memorial Records, 1914–1918.* It also holds the Francis Joseph Bigger collection that includes rare books and bound manuscripts dealing with the Irish regiments in the service of France during the 1700s. British military periodicals held in the General Reference library include the *Air Force List* (1935 onwards), *Army List* (1811), *Navy List* (1915 onwards), *Illustrated War News* (1914–1918) and *Army and Navy Illustrated* (1895–1905). There are also collections of *Journal of the Society for Army Historical Research* and the *Irish Sword*, the journal of the Military History Society of Ireland.

Carlow County Library
Tullow Street, Carlow. Tel: 0593 9170094 E-mail carlowlib@ireland.com

Cavan County Library
Farnham Street, Cavan. Tel: 049 4331799 E-mail cavancountylibrary@tinet.ie

Chester Beatty Library
The Clock Tower Building, Dublin Castle, Dublin 2. Tel: 01 4070750 E-mail info@cbl.ie Web www.cbl.ie/
The library holds the 'Regiments of the British Army' series in the regimental bindings.

Clare County Library HQ
Mill Road, Ennis, County Clare. Tel: 065 6846271E-mail mailbox@clarelibrary.ie Web http://www.clarelibrary.ie

Cork City Library
Grand Parade, Cork. Tel: 021 4277110 E-mail citylibrary@corkcorp.ie Web http://www.corkcitylibrary.ie
As well as general military titles and publications, such as the *Journal of the Cork Historical and Archaeological Society,* the library holds a number of rare titles including the *Record of the North Cork Regiment of Militia* and the *Regimental Records of the 3rd Battalion Royal Munster Fusiliers.*

Cork County Library HQ
Farranlea Road, Cork. Tel: 021 4546499 E-mail corkcountylibrary@eircom.net Web http://www.corkcoco.com/ccmm/services/library/index.htm

Derry Central Library
Foyle Street, Derry City. Tel: 028 71272300 E-mail foyle.street@hotmail.com

Donegal County Library
Administrative Centre, Rosemount, Letterkenny, County Donegal. Tel: 074 9121968 E-mail Library@donegalcoco.ie
The library's special collection has a section on Peadar O'Donnell, com-

mander of the IRA in north east Donegal during the War of Independence and activist on the anti-Treaty side in the Civil War. Also available is a collection relating to Patrick MacGill, the Donegal novelist who served with the London Irish Rifles during the First World War and wrote several books on life in the trenches.

Dublin Public Libraries Information and Cultural Heritage Services
Cumberland House, Fenian Street, Dublin 2. Tel: 01 6619000 E-mail Dublin.city.libs@iol.ie Web www.iol.ie/resource/dublincitylibrary

Dun Laoghaire-Rathdown County Library
Duncairn House (1st floor), 14 Carysfort Avenue, Blackrock, County Dublin. Tel: 01 2781788 E-mail libraries@dlrcoco.ie Web www.dlrcoco.ie/library
The library holds a collection of front pages of the national press, and pro- and anti-Treaty newspapers from the Civil War period.

Fingal County Library HQ
County Hall, Swords, County Dublin. Tel: 01 8905524 E-mail libraries@fingalcoco.ie Web http://www.fingalcoco.ie

Galway County Library HQ
Island House, Cathedral Square, Galway. Tel: 091 562471/565039 E-mail info@galwaylibrary.ie Web http://indigo.ie/~gallibr

Gilbert Library/Dublin City Archives
138/142 Pearse Street, Dublin 2. Tel: 01 6744888 (Archives); 01 6744999 (Gilbert L.) E-mail dubcoll@iol.ie
This library holds extensive collections of national and radical political newspapers and the Gilbert collection relating to the history of Dublin. Now part of the refurbished Dublin City Archives, with a new 100-seater research reading room.

Irish Labour History Museum and Archives
Beggars Bush, Haddington Road, Dublin 4. Tel: 01 6681071 E-mail ilhm@dna.ie
The ILHS library contains books relating to the labour movement during the War of Independence and Irish volunteers for the Spanish republic as well as more general Irish historical works.
Access by appointment.

Kerry County Library HQ
Moyderwell, Tralee, County Kerry. Tel: 066 7121200 E-mail kerrycolibrary@eircom.net Web www.kerrycountylibrary.com
The special collections section of the library has material relating to Thomas Ashe, the Kerry-born leader of the Ashbourne ambush during the 1916 Rising, who died on hunger strike in 1917. There is also a collection on Roger Casement, who was captured while attempting to bring German guns ashore in Kerry at Easter 1916.

Kildare County Library HQ
Athgarvan Road, Droichead Nua (Newbridge), County Kildare. Tel: 045 431486/431109 E-mail kildarelibrary@kildarecoco.ie Web http://www.kildare.ie/library/library/index.html

Kildare History and Family Research Centre
Riverbank, Newbridge, County Kildare. Tel: 045 433602/431611E-mail kildarelocalhistory@eircom.net
The Local Studies department has some publications and journals dealing with the history of the Curragh camp and army barracks. It also holds local newspapers on microfilm.

Kilkenny County Library HQ
6, John's Quay, Kilkenny Tel: 056 7722021/7722606 E-mail katlibs@iol.ie Web http://www.kilkennycoco.ie
The Local Studies department has numerous sources relating to various conflicts, including the rebellions of 1798, 1848 and 1867, the 1916–23 period, the two world wars and Irish United Nations missions. The material is contained in books, journal articles, files and newspaper extracts. Among the local journals of interest are the *Old Kilkenny Review* and *Decies–Old Waterford Society*. Newspaper sources are available on microfilm in the Local Studies department.

Laois County Library HQ
County Library, Kea-Lew Business Park, Portlaoise, County Laois. Tel: 0502 72340/41 E-mail library@laoiscoco.ie
There are a small number of files relating to military activity in the library.

Leitrim County Library
Ballinamore, County Leitrim. Tel: 078 44012 Fax: 078 44425 E-mail leitrimlibrary@eircom.net
The Local Studies section of the library contains numerous items of military interest. There are press cuttings, files and journal articles (especially in *Breifne*) on local involvement in the 1798 Rebellion and the subsequent French landings in the west as well as material on the Spanish Armada and the American Civil War. There is a substantial amount of material on Leitrim and Longford men's service in World War One. The collection also includes autograph books, internment orders and memoirs of the War of Independence and Civil War periods, especially dealing with the Selton Hill ambush of 1921 in which six IRA volunteers were killed.

Limerick City Library
The Granary, Michael Street, Limerick. Tel: 061 314668/415799 E-mail citylib@limerickcorp.ie Web http://www.limerickcorp.ie/library/ main.htm
This library holds several books related to Limerick's role in military history and the journal of the Royal Munster Fusiliers Association. The library's collection of the *Old Limerick Journal* is a significant source for military heritage, especially that related to the Limerick region. The 1990 edition was a special devoted to the 1690 siege, for example. The library has a collection of *Limerick War News* dating from the Civil War. Another important source is a list of all military references in the Limerick city trade directories, 1769–1879.

Limerick County Library HQ
58 O'Connell Street, Limerick. Tel: 061 214452 E-mail colibrar@limerickcoco.ie
The library holds a full set of the *Old Limerick Journal,* that features extensive coverage of military history. Articles relate particularly to matters of Limerick or mid-west interest and include 'Limerick and the Spanish Civil War', 'The Royal Munster Fusiliers, 1914–1918', 'The Munsters in South Africa, 1899–1902', 'The Limerick City Militia, 1798',and the 'Defences of Ireland, 1793–1815: the Shannon Estuary'.

Linen Hall Library, Belfast
17 Donegall Square North, Belfast BT1 5GB. Tel: 028 90321707 E-mail info@linenhall.com Web http://www.linenhall.com

The library holds an extensive collection of books, periodicals and newspapers relating to the history of Belfast. It was founded in 1788 and one of its first librarians was the United Irishman, Thomas Russell. The library has substantial collections relating to the 1798 period, as well as the Northern Ireland Political Collection, the single most important archive of the conflict from 1969 onwards. The Political Collection contains over 11,500 books and documents, 2,000 periodicals and 75,000 other items.
For information on this collection contact y.murphy@linenhall.com

Longford County Library HQ
Town Centre, Longford. Tel: 043 41124/41125 E-mail longlib@iol.ie
The library holds record books of the County Longford militia (1783–1855) and the list of Longford-born soldiers killed in action while serving with British regiments in the Great War. It also has a limited number of statements by local activists in the War of Independence.

Louth County Library
Roden Place, Dundalk, County Louth. Tel: 042 9353190 Fax: 042 9337635
The library holds an extensive collection of journals and locally produced histories including two on the Louth Rifles (1854–1908). Publications such as the *Louth Archaeological Journal*, *Journal of Old Drogheda* and *Tempest's Annual* carrying articles on subjects as diverse as Dundalk soldiers killed in the First World War, and Louth Wild Geese veterans in the French Army during the 1700s are also available. The library has the twelve volumes of *Ireland's Memorial Records*, which list the Irish dead of the First World War. The special collections section of the library holds a minute book from the Louth Local Defence Force, 1940–1.

Mayo County Library
Mountain View, Castlebar, County Mayo. Tel: 094 9024444 E-mail cbarlib@iol.ie Web http://www.mayo-ireland.ie/Mayo/CoDev/Mayolibs.htm
The library has a collection relating to Mayo's role in the 1798 Rebellion. There is a body of material relating to Michael Davitt, the Fenian and Land League leader and also a limited amount of material relating to the local IRA during the War of Independence.

Meath County Library HQ
Railway Street, Navan, County Meath. Tel: 046 9021451/9021134 E-mail cmangan@meathcoco.ie

Monaghan County Library HQ
The Diamond, Clones, County Monaghan. Tel: 047 51143 E-mail moncolib@eircom.net
The library holds the Marron papers, which contain interviews with local veterans of the revolutionary period.

National Library of Ireland
2/3 Kildare Street, Dublin 2. Tel: 01 6030200 Fax: 01 6766690 E-mail info@nli.ie Web http://www.nli.ie/Default.htm
It is likely that anyone conducting research into Irish military history will have to visit the National Library. There one can access all national and local newspapers, and all journals and periodicals published in Ireland. Most books published in this country are held in its collections; however, it can take some time for recent publications to become available to readers. A major effort is being made to preserve the library's newspaper collection by placing it on microfilm; hence several newspaper collections will be unavailable at any one time. Anyone wishing to use the National Library must apply for a reader's ticket.
Open 10.00am–9.00pm, Mon.–Wed.; 10.00am–5.00pm, Thur.–Fri.; 10.00am–1.00pm, Sat.

North Eastern Education & Library Board
Area Library, 25–31 Demesne Avenue, Ballymena, County Antrim BT43 7BG. Tel: 028 25664100 E-mail neelb@nics.co.uk

Offaly County Library
O'Connor Square, Tullamore, County Offaly. Tel: 0506 46833/46834 E-mail colibrar@offalycoco.ie Web www.offaly.ie
The library holds runs of the region's press and some local journals that contain articles of military interest.

Roscommon County Library HQ
Abbey Street, Roscommon. Tel: 09066 25474 E-mail roslib@eircom.net Web http://ireland.iol.ie/~roslib

Sligo County Library HQ
Westward Town Centre, Bridge Street, Sligo. Tel: 071 47190/55060 E-mail sligolib@iol.ie

The library holds a number of statements by local veterans of the War of Independence and Civil War as well as Sinn Féin minute books from the same period. It also has microfilmed miscellaneous records of the Sligo militia, 1856–77.

South Dublin County Library
Unit 1, The Square Industrial Complex, Tallaght, Dublin 24. Tel: 01 4597834 E-mail talib@sdublincoco.ie Web http://www.sdcc.ie/communit.htm

Southern Eastern Education and Library Board
Windmill Hill, Ballynahinch, County Down BT24 8DH. Tel: 028 97566400 E-mail ref@branchlibhq.demon.co.uk

Southern Education and Library Board
HQ, 1 Markethill Road, Armagh BT60 1NR. Tel: 028 37525353 E-mail selb.Armagh.xx@campus.bt.com

Tipperary Joint Libraries Committee
County Library, Castle Avenue, Thurles, County Tipperary. Tel: 0504 23442 E-mail tipplibs@iol.ie Web http://ireland.iol.ie/~tipplibs/
Among the relevant material are several books on local participation in conflict including the records of the Tipperary Artillery (1793–1889) and a list of officers, a short history of Tipperary Military Barracks and back issues of the *Tipperary Historical Journal*. There is also a limited number of statements by local veterans of the War of Independence.

Waterford County Library HQ
Main Street, Lismore, County Waterford. Tel: 058 54128 E-mail ebhqcirc@iol.ie
The library holds a database of those who died serving during the First World War, along with a list of the County Waterford dead of that war.

Waterford Municipal Library HQ
Lady Lane, Waterford. Tel: 051 309975 E-mail colibrar@waterfordcorp.ie

Westmeath County Library HQ
Dublin Road, Mullingar, County Westmeath. Tel: 044 40781 E-mail iflynn@westmeathcoco.ie

The library holds the Howard Bury collection; Colonel Howard Bury's PoW diaries of World War I are conserved in Trinity College Library, Dublin.

Western Education & Library Board
Library HQ, 1 Spillars Place, Omagh, County Tyrone BT78 1HL. Tel: 048 82244821 E-mail librarian@omalib.demon.co.uk

Wexford County Library
Library Management Services, Kents Building, Ardcavan, Wexford. Tel: 053 24922/24928 E-mail libraryhq@wexfordcoco.ie Web http://www.wexford.ie/library.htm
The library holds an extensive collection relating to the 1798 Rebellion.

Wicklow County Library HQ
UDC Offices, Boghall Road, Bray, County Wicklow. Tel: 01 2866566
E-mail wcchq@tinet.ie

OTHER INSTITUTIONS

Many schools and other institutions house records that are relevant to military heritage. Often school magazines feature rolls of honour or reports of past pupils' service in wartime. Many private institutions, such as banks, will also have recorded the contribution of their staff to military service and many head offices of Irish banks have compiled memorials to honour staff that fought in the world wars.

Allied Irish Banks plc
3–4 Foster Place, Dublin 2. Tel: 01 6776721
Enquiries by post *only*.

Bank of Ireland
Head Office, Lower Baggot Street, Dublin 2. Tel: 01 6615933
The bank holds a First World War staff service record.
Enquiries by post *only*.

Belvedere College SJ
Museum and archive, 6 Great Denmark Street, Dublin 1. Tel: 01 6586636
Fax: 01 8744374

This new museum and archive contains information on former pupils' service with both the Irish and British armed forces. Among past pupils was Kevin Barry, the IRA Volunteer executed in November 1920. Records begin in 1832.
Enquiries by post.

Clongowes Wood College
Naas, County Kildare. Tel: 045 868202 E-mail reception@clongowes.net
The collection of the *Clongownian* annual includes issues from 1917, 1918 and 1919 which outline past pupils' service during the First World War.
Enquiries by post *only*.

St Patrick's College
Thurles, County Tipperary. Tel: 0504 21201/24466 E-mail luceat@eircom.net
A small amount of biographical material is available on priests from the archdiocese who served as chaplains during the First World War. The papers of Fr Michael Maher contain a diary on events during the War of Independence.
Enquiries by post.

Most of the following bodies are primarily concerned with the welfare of serving or former service people. A number of them do engage in historical research themselves and/or can aid a researcher.

American Legion (Ireland)
John F. Kennedy Post, Web www.jfkamerleg-irlpost63.com c/o 71 Foxfield Road, Raheny, Dublin. 5. Tel: 01 8317792
Fr Duffy Post, Web http://www.geocities.com/frduffypost/ c/o Glen Foy, Killeen, Corofin, County Clare. Tel: 065 6837863
An organization for ex-members of the United States armed services.

An Cosantóir
The Defence Forces Magazine, DFHQ, Parkgate, Dublin 8. Tel: 01 8042691 Fax: 01 6779018 E-mail ancosantoir@defenceforces.iol.ie
Published monthly, *An Cosantóir* contains articles of military interest including regular features on military history.

Bandon War Memorial Committee
23 Oliver Plunkett Street, Bandon, County Cork E-mail billygood@eircom.net Web www.bandonmemorial.com

Brú na bhFiann (Home for ex-Members of the Defence Forces)
17–19 Queen Street, Dublin 7. Tel: 01 8729261 Fax: 01 8729516

Combined Irish Regiments Association
E-mail contact@combined-irish-regiments-oca.co.uk Web www.combined-irish-regiments-oca.co.uk/
The association is dedicated to keeping alive the heritage of all the Irish regiments of the British armed forces, past and present.

Connaught Rangers Association
The Secretary, Connaught Rangers Association, King House, Main Street, Boyle, County Roscommon.

Garda Historical Society
c/o Garda Museum, The Records Tower, Dublin Castle, Dublin 2. Tel: 01 6719597 Web www.esatclear.ie/~garda/index.html

Irish Brigade Association
E-mail laverty@optonline.net
The service of the Irish in United States forces.

Irish Regiments Historical Society
21 Helen's Park, 'Aghalee', Craigavon, County Armagh BT 67 OEN
The society seeks to commemorate Irish regiments through a programme of talks and field trips.

Irish United Nations Veterans Association
Arbour House, Mount Temple Road, Dublin 7. Tel: 01 6791262 E-mail: iunvapost@iolfree.i

Irish Veterans Memorial Project
Administration office: Capel Chambers, 119 Capel Street, Dublin 1. E-mail info@irishveteransmemorial.com Web www.irishveteransmemorial.com
This project seeks to establish a memorial to Irish veterans of conflict in the twentieth century. It is to be based in a exhibition and research centre at Kiltoom, outside Athlone.

Irish Vietnam Veterans Association
c/o IVMP, Capel Chambers, 119 Capel Street, Dublin 1.

Lebanon War Veterans Organisation (Ireland)
57 Upper Dorset Street, Dublin 1. Tel: 01 8656638 Fax: 01 8749253
E-mail: office@lebwarvets.org Web: www.lebwarvets.org

Military History Society of Ireland
Newman House, University College, 86 St Stephen's Green, Dublin 2.
The society was founded in 1949. Its purpose is to further the study of Irish military history and, in particular, the history of warfare in Ireland and Irish people engaged in war. Members receive its journal, the *Irish Sword,* twice yearly. The society holds monthly lectures in Griffith College, Dublin, and organizes summer field trips and overseas tours.

National Graves Association
PO Box 7105, 74 Dame Street, Dublin 2. Tel: 01 8621928 & 087 2282033
The NGA was founded in 1926 to maintain and restore the graves and memorials of Irish republican dead of every generation. At present, over 500 memorials and graves are in the NGA's care. From June to September, the NGA organizes free guided walking tours of Dublin's Glasnevin Cemetery.

Organisation of National Ex-Servicemen and Women
17 Queen Street, Dublin 7. Tel: 01 8729549 Fax: 01 8729261

Robert Emmet Association
27 Pearse Street, Dublin 2. Tel: 01 6776593 E-mail emmet200@eircom.net

Royal British Legion
Head Office, 26 South Frederick Street, Dublin 2. Tel: 01 6713044 *also* 3 Crosthwaite Terrace, Dun Laoghaire. Tel: 2805536
A welfare organisation.

Royal British Legion Club
4 Sir John Rogerson Quay, Dublin 2. Tel: 01 6793036

Royal British Legion Northern Ireland
War Memorial Buildings, 9–13 Waring Street, Belfast BT 1 2EV. Tel: 028

90321683 Fax: 028 90330782 E-mail wcraig@britishlegion.org.uk
The Royal British Legion was founded in 1921 to look after the welfare and interests of British ex-servicemen. It is most popularly associated with the sale of the Poppy each November. Membership is open to all who have served with the British armed forces, while others who support the Legion's work can obtain associate membership.

Royal Dublin Fusiliers Association
The Secretary, RDFA, Dublin Civic Museum, 58 South William Street, Dublin 2. E-mail **rdfa@eircom.net**

Royal Ulster Constabulary GC Historical Society
c/o Police Museum, Headquarters Police Service of Northern Ireland, 'Brocklyn', 65 Knock Road, Belfast BT5 6LE. Tel: 028 90700116

The Somme Association
233 Bangor Road, Newtownards, County Down BT23 7PH. Tel: 028 91823202 Fax: 028 91823214 E-mail Sommeassociation@dnet.co.uk Web www.irishsoldier.org

UK National Inventory of War Memorials
Imperial War Museum, Lambeth Road, London SE1 6HZ.
Tel: 0044 20 7416 5353 E-mail memorials@iwm.org.uk

TOURS

Military Heritage Tours Ltd
Military Heritage Tours, Woodfield, Derryhick, Castlebar, County Mayo. Tel: 094 9031344 E-mail dbuckley@anu.ie Web www.militaryheritagetours.com
This company organizes guided tours of Irish battlefields and military heritage. Tours have included west Cork during the War of Independence, a Williamite War tour of the midlands and a 1798 tour of the west.

1916 Walking Tours of Dublin
Tel: 01 473 4986 E-mail 1916@indigo.ie web www.1916rising.com/
These tours recount the story of the 1916 Easter Rising. Tour groups meet during summer at 11.30am and 2.30pm at the International Bar, 23 Wicklow Street, Dublin 2.

Historical Walking Tours of Dublin
Tel: 01 8780227 Fax: 01 8783787 E-mail tours@historicalinsights.ie Web www.historicalinsights.ie
This regular walking tour includes sites of military interest such as Dublin Castle, the House of Lords and Trinity College. A special tour entitled 'A Terrible Beauty', dedicated to the 1916 23 period, is also available through this popular walking tour company. Tours leave the front gates of Trinity College daily.

Irish Historical Tours
Tel: 028 90596217 E-mail info@irishhistoricaltours.com Web www.irish-historicaltours.com
Tours include Emmet's Rebellion, the Williamite War and Cork's Fighting Story.

Rebel Dublin Tours
c/o Tar Isteach, 40/41 Lower Dominick Street, Dublin 1. Tel: 01 8749990/ 087 2275657 E-mail treacyma@tcd.ie
This walking tour explores rebel Dublin, from the 1913 lockout, through the Easter Rising, the War of Independence and the Civil War. Tour groups meet daily during summer at the Abbey Hotel, Abbey Street, at 11.00am and alongside Larkin's Statue on O'Connell Street at 2.45pm.

The world-wide web

The world-wide web is a major resource for those embarking on research and the following is a guide to sites relevant to Irish military history as of June 2003. Where possible, it has been noted where a website is that of an institution or official body, or the work of an enthusiast, which may be less authoritative. It is also important to note that unofficial sites often change address or simply disappear without notice. These sites provide a gateway to other relevant sources. An extensive guide to relevant websites is provided by the Military Heritage of Ireland Trust Limited at http://www.irishsoldiers.com/links.html

MEMORIAL SITES

Australian War Memorial
www.awm.gov.au/index.asp
The official Australian government site, it includes a roll of honour of every Australian killed in the line of duty since the Boer War.

Athy, County Kildare, World War One Dead
http://kildare.ie/hospitality/historyandheritage/AthyHeritage/ww1.htm
Unofficial site.

Ballymoney, County Antrim, World War One Dead
http://www.ballymoneyheroes.co.uk/
Unofficial site.

Bandon, County Cork, Memorial Committee
http://www.bandonmemorial.com/
Unofficial site.

Canadian Virtual War Memorial
http://www.virtualmemorial.gc.ca/
This official site contains the names of 116,000 Canadians and Newfoundlanders who died in the service of their country.

Commonwealth War Graves Commission
http://www.cwgc.org
This official site lists the names of all those who died in British or Commonwealth service, 1914–21 and 1939–47.

Emmet 200
http://homepage.eircom.net/~emmet200/

Irish Korean War Dead
www.illyria.com/korwar.html
This unofficial site records the Irish dead of the 1950–3 conflict.

Irish Rebels to Australia, 1797–1806
http://www.tip.net.au/~ppmay/rebels.htm
Database and links detailing the deportation of captured United Irish rebels to Australia.

Irish Vietnam War Dead
http://www.illyria.com/vn_irish_names.html
This unofficial site includes Irish dead of both US and Australian forces.

Journey of Reconciliation and Trust
http://www.iol.ie/jrtrust
This site was established by those involved in the Messines Peace Tower project of 1998.

New Zealand Armed Forces Memorial Project
www.nzafmp.org/
A project which aims to compile lists of New Zealand's war dead available on line.

North Clare World War One Dead
http://www.clarelibrary.ie/eolas/coclare/history/soldiers/north_clare_soldiers.htm
This local commemorative site is maintained by Clare County Library.

Remembering Robert Emmet, 1778–1803
http://www.robertemmet.org/

Tipperary World War One Dead
http://hompage.eircom.net/~tipperaryfame
Unofficial commemorative site.

Battles in Irish History
http://website.lineone.net/~bonzytwo/timeline.html.htm
A chronology of Irish battles.

Battle of Clontarf, 1014
http://www.bbc.co.uk/history/timelines/ni/battle_clontarf.shtml
A BBC history site.

Corpus of Irish electronic texts
http://www.ucc.ie/celt
Features on-line historical texts, particularly related to medieval Ireland.

De Re Militari
http://www.deremilitari.org
A European medieval warfare society site, with extensive links.

Edward Bruce in Ireland
http://www.bbc.co.uk/history/timelines/ni/defeat_edward_bruce.shtml
A BBC history site that explains the background to the Bruce invasions of Ireland, 1315–18.

Gallowglass
http://www.cisl.ie/mars/rory/gallowglass.htm
An enthusiast's site dedicated to the Scots mercenaries in medieval Ireland.

Ireland's history in maps
http://www.rootsweb.com/~ir/kik/ihm/iremaps.htm
This site includes many maps of military interest.

Irish arms
http://www.irisharms.ie
This site provides links to medieval re-enactment and living history groups.

Norman invasion
http://www.bbc.co.uk/history/timelines/ni/normans.shtml
This BBC history site explores the Anglo-Norman invasion of Ireland from 1169.

The battle of Dysert O'Dea
http://members.tripod.com/~rodea/history.htm
A site concerning warfare between Anglo-Normans and Clare chieftains in 1318.

The Normans in Thomond
http://www.clarelibrary.ie/eolas/coclare/history/norman.htm
A Clare County Library site describing Norman rule in Munster.

Shane O'Neill's rebellion
http://www.bbc.co.uk/history/timelines/ni/shane_o_neill.shtml
The Ulster chieftain's wars of the 1560s are dealt with here.

Conflict in Carlow
http://carlow.local.ie/content/10371.shtml/history/general
A local site describing warfare in the county from 1641 to 1798.

The battle of Benburb
http://www.scotwars.com/html/battle_of-benburb.htm
This site covers O'Neill's 1646 victory over General Munroe.

The Spanish Armada
http://www.clarelibrary.ie/eolas/coclare/history/spanish_armada.htm
A Clare County Library site on the attempted 1588 invasion of Ireland.

The battle of Kinsale
http://www.bbc.co.uk/history/bytime/ni/battle_kinsale.shtml
A BBC history site on the decisive defeat of Gaelic forces in 1602.

The 1641 Rebellion
http://www.bbc.co.uk/history/timelines/ni/rebellion_1641.shtml
This deals with one of one of the bloodiest rebellions in Irish history.

The battle of Aughrim
http://www.local.ie/general/history/williamite/aughrim/index.shtml
The key victory of the Williamite forces in 1691 is explored here.

The battle of the Boyne, 1690
http://www.local.ie/general/history/williamite/boyne/index.shtml
This investigates the background to the most famous battle in Irish history.

The siege of Derry
http://www.bbc.co.uk/history/bytime/ni/siege_derry.shtml
This deals with the successful defence of Derry by the Williamites in 1689.

The 1798 Rebellion
http://www.local.ie/general/history/1798/index.shtml
This is an index of links to sites documenting the bloodiest rebellion in modern Irish history.

1798 links
http://www.iol.ie/~fagann/1798/
Another set of documentary links.

1798 facsimile documents
http://www.nationalarchives.ie/1798intro.html
This presents a collection of contemporary documents produced by the National Archives of Ireland.

Local 1798 sites

Clare *see* via www.clarelibrary.ie

Kildare http://www.local.ie/general/history/1798/leinster_rising.shtml

Mayo http://www.local.ie/general/history/1798/mayo/index.shtml

Ulster http://www.local.ie/general/history/1798/ulster/index.shtml

Wexford http://www.local.ie/general/history/1798wexford/index.shtml

History of the Irish Defence Forces
http://www.military.ie/introduction/history.htm
Official site.

Irish Defence Forces insignia
http://homepage.eircom.net/~irishmiltaryinsignia
This site illustrates contemporary insignia of the Irish Defence Forces.

Irish military insignia
http://indigo.ie/~iesoh
Insignia of Irish Volunteers, Cumann na mBan, Citizen Army and IRA (1913–22) feature at the site.

The Easter Rising
http://www.bbc.co.uk/history/war/easterrising/index.shtml
A BBC site concerning the background to the Easter Rising.

Michael Collins
http://www.iol.ie/~seanhly
This site contains numerous links to sites commemorating the best known leader of the War of Independence.

The Kilmichael ambush
http://www.searcs-web.com/barry3.html
This site recounts the story of the November 1920 ambush of British forces by the west Cork IRA under Tom Barry.

World War Two and Ireland
http://www.csn.ul.ie/~dan/war/eire.htm
This comprehensive site provides information on neutral Ireland's defence effort and attitude to belligerent powers.

The Irish in uniform
http://homepage.tinet.ie/~tipperaryfame/index.html
A Tipperary-based site that commemorates Irish service world wide.

Irish UN service
http://www.military.ie/overseas/index.html
This official site covers United Nations missions of the Defence Forces.

Australian Army History
http://www.army.gov.au/ahu/index.htm
An official Australian Army site.

Canadian Military Heritage Project
http://www.rootsweb.com/~canmil/
This is an excellent site for genealogical research, with numerous links of Irish interest.

Canadian War Museum
http://www.civilization.ca/
The national war museum of Canada.

Combined Irish Regiments Association
http://www.combined-irish-regiments-oca.co.uk
This site details the heritage of the British Army's Irish regiments, past and present.

Irish winners of the Victoria Cross
http://www.chapter-one.com/vc/subnat.asp?nat=8
A list of Irish winners of Britain's highest award for gallantry in wartime may be consulted at this site.

Imperial War Museum
http://www.iwm.org.uk
An excellent site of the UK's national war museum with numerous links.

National Army Museum
http://www.national-army-museum.ac.uk
This museum is dedicated to the history of the British Army prior to the twentieth century.

Royal Dublin Fusiliers Association
http://www.greatwar.ie
Very useful information and links on Irish service in the Great War are available at the site.

British Army Regiments, 1914–1918
http://www.1914-1918.net/regiments.htm
The records of all Irish regiments who served in the First World War can be traced here.

THE AMERICAS

The American Revolution
http://www.americanrevolution.org/home.html
Here one finds numerous links to sites explaining a conflict in which Irish people fought on both sides.

American Society for Military History
http://www.smh-hq.org

Centre for Military History
http://www.army.mil/cmh-pg
Two authoritative sites devoted to US military history.

69th New York
http://www.69thnyvi.homestead.com
One of many Civil War re-enactment sites, with good Irish interest links.

The Irish and the American Civil War
http://216.110.172.115/irish.htm
This site outlines the involvement of the Irish in the conflict.

The 28th Massachusetts Volunteers
http://www.28thmass.org/HistMen/HisMenu.htm
This excellent site devoted to this Irish Union regiment features extensive background information on the social, economic and political aspects of Irish participation on both sides in the Civil War.

The San Patricios
http://www.dayproductions.com/in_distribution
The story of the Irish men who deserted the American Army to fight for Mexico in 1848 is recounted here.

Ireland and the Spanish Civil War
http://members.lycos.co.uk/spanishcivilwar/
This site provides very comprehensive information on the Irish who took opposing sides in the Spanish conflict.

The Irish in other wars and armies
http://www.illyria.com/irish/irishwar.html
This site's links detail Irish participation in warfare in locations as diverse as Argentina and Austria, from the 1700s to the present day.

Wild Geese Heritage Centre
http://indigo.ie/~wildgees/index.htm
This site is dedicated to the history of the Irish who served in European armies during the 1700s.

The Wild Geese today
http://www.thewildgeese.com
This site has extensive Irish military links.

Select bibliography of Irish military history

Researchers undertaking study should begin by consulting the bibliography of *A military history of Ireland* (1996), edited by Thomas Bartlett and Keith Jeffery; this features over 600 relevant books, articles and essays. As of June 2003, *A military history of Ireland* was still available to buy, and it is to be found in most good libraries. However, much has been published since 1996 that adds to our knowledge of Ireland's military heritage. This bibliography is, therefore, heavily biased towards works published (or republished) in the last decade. Much writing on Irish military history appears in specialist journals, many of which are not readily accessible to the general public; the most important is the *Irish Sword*, published twice a year, which is available in over thirty county libraries across Ireland or directly from the Military History Society of Ireland.

GENERAL WORKS

Bartlett, T. and Jeffery, K. (eds), *A military history of Ireland* (Cambridge, 1996).

Bell, J.B., *The secret army: the IRA* (Dublin, 1997).

Blackstock, A., *An ascendancy army: the Irish yeomanry, 1796–1834* (Dublin, 1998).

Clements, B., *Defending the north: the fortifications of Ulster, 1796–1956* (Newtownards, 2003).

Comerford, R.V., *The Fenians in context: Irish politics and society, 1848–82* (Dublin, 1998).

Costello, C., *A most delightful station: the British army on the Curragh of Kildare, Ireland, 1855–1922* (Cork, 1996).

Coogan, T.P., *The IRA* (London, 1996).

Doherty, R., *The sons of Ulster: Ulstermen at war from the Somme to Korea* (Belfast, 1992).

—, *The North Irish Horse: a hundred years of service* (Staplehurst, 2002).

— & Truesdale, D., *Irish winners of the Victoria Cross* (Dublin, 2000).

Dooley, T., *The greatest of the Fenians: John Devoy and Ireland* (Dublin, 2003).

Duffy, S. (ed.), *An atlas of Irish history* (Dublin, 1997).
Dungan, M., *Distant drums: Irish men in foreign armies* (Belfast, 1993).
English, R., *Armed struggle: a history of the IRA* (London, 2003).
Grenham, J., *Tracing your Irish ancestors* (Dublin, 1999).
Harris, R.G., *The Irish regiments: a pictorial history, 1683–1987* (Staplehurst, 1999).
Hayes, McCoy, G., *Irish battles: a military history of Ireland* (Belfast, 1989).
Heath, I. and Sque, D., *The Irish wars, 1485–1603* (London, 1993).
Helferty, S. and Refaussé, R. (eds), *Directory of Irish archives*, 4th edition (Dublin, 2003).
Herlihy, J., *The Dublin Metropolitan Police: a short history and genealogical guide* (Dublin, 2001)
—, *The Royal Irish Constabulary: a complete list of officers and men, 1816–1922* (Dublin, 1999).
—, *The Royal Irish Constabulary: a short history and genealogical guide* (Dublin, 1997).
Irish Guards, *The first hundred years, 1900–2000* (Staplehurst, 2000).
Jourdan, H.F.N. and Fraser, E., *The Connaught Rangers* (Cork, 1999).
Kelleher, G.D., *Gunpowder to guided missiles – Ireland's war industries* (Cork, 1993).
Kerrigan, P.M., *Castles and fortifications in Ireland, 1485–1945* (Cork, 1995).
Le Gretton, G. and Geoghegan, S., *The campaigns and history of the Royal Irish Regiment* (Cork, 1997).
Litton, H., *Irish rebellions, 1798–1916: an illustrated history* (Dublin, 1998).
McCance, R.S., *History of the Royal Munster Fusiliers* (Cork, 1995).
McConville, S., *Irish political prisoners, 1848–1922* (London, 2003).
McGarry, F. (ed.), *Republicanism in modern Ireland* (Dublin, 2003).
O'Halpin, E., *Defending Ireland: the Irish state and its enemies since 1922* (Oxford, 1999).
Reeves-Smyth, T., *Irish castles* (Belfast, 1995).
Townshend, C., *Political violence in Ireland: government and resistance since 1848* (Oxford, 1983).

MEDIEVAL IRELAND

Barry, T.B., *The archaeology of medieval Ireland* (London, 1999).
Duffy, S., *Ireland in the Middle Ages* (Dublin, 1997).
—, *Robert the Bruce's Irish wars: the invasions of Ireland, 1306–1329* (Stroud, Glos., 2002).
Kenyon, J.R. and O'Conor, K. (eds), *The medieval castle in Ireland and Wales* (Dublin, 2003).

McNeill, T., *Castles in Ireland: feudal power in a Gaelic world* (London, 1997).
O'Byrne, E., *War, politics and the Irish of Leinster*, 1156–1606 (Dublin, 2003).
Simms, K., *From kings to warlords* (Woodbridge, 1987).
Smith, B., *Colonisation and conquest in medieval Ireland* (Cambridge, 1999).
Sweetman, D., *The medieval castles of Ireland* (Cork, 1999).

16TH CENTURY

Brady, C., *A viceroy's vindication?: Sir Henry Sidney's memoir of service in Ireland, 1556–78* (Cork, 2001).
Henry, G., *Irish military communities in Spanish Flanders, 1586–1621* (Dublin, 1992).
Morgan, H., *Tyrone's rebellion: the outbreak of the Nine Years War in Tudor Ireland* (London, 1993).

17TH AND 18TH CENTURIES

Doherty, R., *The Williamite War in Ireland, 1688–1691* (Dublin, 1998).
Flanagan, L., *Irish wrecks of the Spanish Armada* (Dublin, 1995).
French, Noel, *The battle of the Boyne* (Trim, 1990).
Litton, H., *Cromwell: an illustrated history* (Dublin, 2000).
Kelly, W. (ed.), *The sieges of Derry* (Dublin, 2001).
Lenihan, P., *Confederate Catholics at war* (Dublin, 2001).
Mac Cuarta, B. (ed.), *Ulster 1641: aspects of the rising* (Belfast, 1993).
Maguire, W. (ed.), *Kings in conflict: the revolutionary war in Ireland and its aftermath, 1689–1750* (Belfast, 1990).
McCavitt, J., *The Flight of the Earls* (Dublin, 2002).
McGurk, J., *The Elizabethan conquest of Ireland* (Manchester, 1997).
McKenny, K., *The Laggan army in Ireland, 1640–80* (Dublin, forthcoming).
Ohlmeyer, J., *Civil war and restoration in the three Stuart kingdoms: the career of Randal MacDonnell* (Dublin, 2001).
— (ed.), *Ireland from independence to occupation, 1641–1660* (Cambridge, 1995).
— (ed.), *The civil wars: a military history of England, Scotland, and Ireland, 1638–1660* (Oxford, 2002).
Ó Ciardha, E., *Ireland and the Jacobite cause, 1685–1766: a fatal attachment* (Dublin, 2002).
Ó Siochrú, M., *Confederate Ireland, 1642–1649* (Dublin, 1999).
— (ed.), *Kingdoms in crisis: Ireland in the 1640s* (Dublin, 2001).
Ó Snodaigh, P., *The Irish Volunteers; a list of the units, 1715–1793* (Dublin, 1995).

Reilly, T., *Cromwell: an honourable enemy* (Kerry, 1999).
Silke, J.J., *Kinsale: the Spanish intervention in Ireland at the end of the Elizabethan wars* (Dublin, 2000).
Stradling, R.A., *The Spanish monarchy and Irish mercenaries, 1618–68* (Dublin, 1993).
Wauchope, P., *Patrick Sarsfield and the Williamite War* (Dublin, 1992).
Wheeler, J. S., *Cromwell in Ireland* (Dublin, 1999).
Wiggins, K., *Anatomy of a siege: King John's Castle, Limerick, 1642* (Bray, 2000).

THE 1798 & 1803 REBELLIONS

Barry, J.M., *Pitchcap and triangle: the Cork Militia in the Wexford Rising* (Cork, 1998).
Bartlett, T., Dickson, D., Keogh, D. and Whelan, K. (eds), *1798: a bicentennial perspective* (Dublin, 2003).
Beatty, J.D., *Protestant women's narratives of the Irish rebellion of 1798* (Dublin, 2001).
Chambers, L., *Rebellion in Kildare, 1798–1803* (Dublin, 1998).
Corrigan, M., *All that delirium of the brave: Kildare in 1798* (Kildare, 1998).
Cullen, S. and Geissel, H. (eds), *Fugitive warfare: 1798 in north Kildare* (Kildare, 1998).
Dickson, C., *The revolt in the north* (London, 1997).
—, *The Wexford rising in 1798* (London, 1998).
Dickson, D., Keogh, D. and Whelan, K. (eds), *The United Irishmen* (Dublin, 1993).
Doyle, E., *The Wexford insurgents of '98 and their march into Meath* (Meath, 1998).
Flynn, K. and McCormack, S., *Westmeath 1798: a Kilbeggan rebellion* (Westmeath, 1998).
Gahan, D., *The people's rising: Wexford 1798* (Dublin, 1995).
Geoghegan, P., *Robert Emmet: a life* (Dublin, 2002).
Hill, M., Turner, B. and Dawson, K., *1798 Rebellion in Co. Down* (Down, 1998).
Kelly, L., *A flame now quenched: rebels and Frenchmen in Leitrim, 1793–1798* (Dublin, 1998).
Keogh, D. and Furlong, N. (eds), *The mighty wave: the 1798 Rebellion in Wexford* (Dublin, 1998).
—, *The women of 1798* (Dublin, 1998).
McHugh, R. (ed.), *Voice of rebellion: Carlow in 1798* (Dublin, 1998).
O'Donnell, R. (ed.), *Insurgent Wicklow 1798: the story as written by Luke Cullen O.D.C.* (Bray, 1998).
—, *The rebellion in Wicklow* (Dublin, 1998).
—, *Aftermath-post rebellion insurgency in Wicklow, 1799–1803* (Dublin, 2000).

—, *Robert Emmet and the Rising of 1803* (Dublin, 2003).
—, *Robert Emmet and the Rebellion of 1798* (Dublin, 2003).
—, *Remember Emmet: images of the life and legacy of Robert Emmet* (Dublin, 2003).
Ó Loinsigh, S., *The 1798 rebellion in Meath* (Meath, 1997).
O'Shaughnessy, P. (ed.), *Rebellion in Wicklow: General Holt's personal account of 1798* (Dublin, 1998).
Power, P., *The courts martial of 1798–1799* (Carlow, 1997).
Quinn, J., *Soul on fire: a life of Thomas Russell, 1767–1803* (Dublin, 2002).
Stewart, A.T.Q., *The summer soldiers: the 1798 Rebellion in Antrim and Down* (Belfast, 1995).
Thompson, F. G., *The uniforms of 1798–1803* (Dublin, 1998).
Turner, B.S., *A man stepped out for death: Thomas Russell and County Down* (Newtownards, 2003).
Tyrell, J., *Weather and warfare: a climatic history of the 1798 Rebellion* (Dublin, 2001).
Ulster Local Studies, *The turbulent decade: Ulster in the 1790s* (Belfast, 1997).
Whelan, K., *The tree of liberty* (Cork, 1996).
—, *Fellowship of freedom* (Cork, 1997).
Wilsdon, B., *Sites of the 1798 Rising in Antrim and Down* (Belfast, 1997).

THE CRIMEAN WAR

Luddy, M. (ed.), *The Crimean journals of the Sisters of Mercy, 1854–6* (Dublin, forthcoming).
Murphy, D., *Ireland and the Crimean war* (Dublin, 2002).

THE BOER WAR

Cassidy, M., *Inniskilling diaries, 1899–1903: 1st battalion, 27th Royal Inniskilling Fusiliers in South Africa* (Barnsley, 2001).
McCracken, D.P., *MacBride's brigade: Irish commandos in the Anglo-Boer War* (Dublin, 1999).

THE FIRST WORLD WAR

Bandon Memorial Committee, *Bandon and district and the First World War* (Bandon, 1996).
Bourke, J. (ed.), *The misfit soldier: Edward Casey's war story, 1914–1918* (Cork, 1999).
Bowman, T., *The Irish regiments in the Great War: discipline and morale* (Manchester, 2003).

Boyce, D.G., *The sure confusing drum: Ireland and the First World War* (Swansea, 1993).

Canning, W.J., *Ballyshannon, Belcoo, Bertincourt: the history of the 11th battalion The Royal Inniskilling Fusiliers (Donegal and Fermanagh Volunteers) in World War One* (Antrim, 1996).

Cooper, B., *The 10th (Irish) Division at Gallipoli* (Dublin, 1993).

Denman, T., *Ireland's unknown soldiers: the 16th (Irish) Division in the Great War* (Dublin, 1992).

—, *A lonely grave: the life and death of William Redmond* (Dublin, 1995).

Doherty, R., *Irish generals: Irish generals in the British Army in the Second World War* (Belfast, 1993).

Dooley, T.P., *Irishmen or English soldiers?: the times and world of a southern Catholic Irishman (1876–1916) enlisting in the British army during the First World War* (Liverpool, 1995).

Dungan, M., *Irish voices from the Great War* (Dublin, 1995).

—, *They shall not grow old: Irish soldiers and the Great War* (Dublin, 1997).

Durney, J., *Far from the short grass: Kildare men in two world wars* (Kildare, 1999).

Fitzpatrick, D. (ed.), *Ireland and the First World War* (Dublin, 1986).

Gregory, A. and Paseta, S. (eds), *Ireland and the Great War: a war to unite us all?* (Manchester, 2002).

Harte, P., *County Donegal book of honour: the Great War, 1914–1918* (Donegal, 2002).

Hennessey, T., *Dividing Ireland: World War I and partition* (London, 1998).

Irish National War Memorial, *Ireland's memorial records, 1914–1918* (8 vols, Dublin, 1923).

Jeffery, K., *Ireland and the Great War* (Cambridge, 2000).

Jervis, H.S., *The 2nd Munsters in France* (Cork, 1998).

Johnstone, T., *Orange, green and khaki: the story of the Irish regiments in the Great War, 1914–1918* (Dublin, 1992).

Kipling, R., *The Irish Guards in the Great War* (Staplehurst, 1997).

Mac Fhionnghaile, N., *Donegal, Ireland and the First World War* (Letterkenny, 1987).

McGuinn, J., *Sligo men in the Great War, 1914–1918* (Sligo, 1994).

Mitchell, G.S., *'Three cheers for the Derrys': a history of the 10th Royal Inniskilling Fusiliers in the 1914–1918 War* (Derry, 1991).

Orr, P., *The road to the Somme: men of the Ulster Division tell their story* (Belfast, 1987).

Robertson, D., *Deeds not words: Irish soldiers, sailors and airmen in two world wars* (Westmeath, 1998).

Sheen, J., *Tyneside Irish: a history of the Tyneside Irish Brigade … in Northumberland in World War One* (Barnsley, 1998).

Spencer, W., *Army service records of the First World War* (London, 2002).
Stokes, R., *Death in the Irish Sea* (Cork, 1998).
Taylor, J., *The 1st Royal Irish Rifles in the Great War* (Dublin, 2002).
Thompson, R., *Bushmills heroes, 1914–1918* (Coleraine, 1994).
United Kingdom War Office, *Soldiers who died in the Great War, 1914–1919*, 80 parts (London 1981: facsimile edition, 1988).

THE REVOLUTIONARY PERIOD (1916–1923) AND AFTER

Abbott, R., *Police casualties in Ireland, 1919–1922* (Dublin, 2000).
Allen Library Project, *Mud Island: a history of Ballybough* (Dublin, 2002).
Andrews, C.S., *Dublin made me: an autobiography* (Dublin, 2001).
—, *Man of no property* (Dublin, 2001).
Augusteijn, J. (ed.), *The Irish revolution, 1913–1923* (Basingstoke, 2002).
—, *From public defiance to guerrilla warfare: the experience of ordinary Volunteers in the Irish War of Independence, 1916–1921* (Dublin, 1996).
Babington, A., *The devil to pay: the mutiny of the Connaught Rangers, July 1920* (Barnsley, 1991).
Barrett, J.J., *In the name of the game* (Dublin, 1997).
Barry, T., *Guerrilla days in Ireland* (Dublin, 1981).
Barton, B., *From behind a closed door: secret court martial records of the Easter 1916 Rising* (Belfast, 2002).
Bennet, R., *The Black and Tans* (New York, 1995).
Breen, D., *My fight for Irish freedom* (Dublin, 1981).
Brennan-Whitmore, W.J., *Dublin burning: the Easter Rising from behind the barricades* (Dublin, 1996).
Carey, T., *Hanged for Ireland* (Dublin, 2001).
Coleman, M., *County Longford and the Irish revolution, 1910–1923* (Dublin, 2002).
Coogan, T.P., *Michael Collins* (London, 1991).
— and Morrison, G., *The Irish Civil War* (London, 1999).
—, *1916: The Easter Rising* (London, 2002).
Costello, F., *The Irish revolution and its aftermath, 1916–1923* (Dublin, 2002).
Deasy, L., *Brother against brother* (Cork, 1998).
—, *Towards Ireland free* (Cork, 2000).
Doherty, G. and Keogh, D. (eds), *Michael Collins and the making of the Irish state* (Cork, 1998).
Dolan, A., *Commemorating the Irish Civil War: history and memory, 1923–2000* (Oxford, 2003).
Doyle, J., Clarke, F., Connaughton, E., and Somerville, O., *An introduction to the Bureau of Military History, 1913–1921* (Dublin, 2003).

Durney, J., *On the one road: political unrest in Kildare, 1913–1994* (Kildare, 2001).
Dwyer, T. Ryle., *Michael Collins: 'the man who won the war'* (Cork, 1990).
—, *Big fellow, long fellow* (Dublin, 1999).
—, *Tans, terror and troubles: Kerry's real fighting story 1913–23* (Cork, 2001).
English, R., *Ernie O'Malley, IRA intellectual* (Oxford, 1998).
English, R. and O'Malley, C., *Prisoners: the Civil War letters of Ernie O'Malley* (Dublin, 1991).
Farry, M., *Sligo 1921–23: the aftermath of revolution* (Dublin, 2000).
Fitzpatrick, D. (ed.), *Revolution?: Ireland, 1917–1923* (Dublin, 1990).
—, *Politics and Irish life, 1913–1921* (Cork, 1998).
—, *Harry Boland's Irish revolution* (Cork, 2003).
Foy, M. and Barton, B., *The Easter Rising* (Surrey, 1999).
Gallagher, R., *Violence and nationalist politics in Derry City, 1920–1923* (Dublin, 2003).
Good, J., *Enchanted by dreams: the journal of a revolutionary, Joe Good* (Dingle, 1996).
Griffith, K., and O'Grady, T., *Curious journey: an oral history of Ireland's unfinished revolution* (Cork, 1998).
Hanley, B., *The IRA, 1926–1936* (Dublin, 2002).
Harnett, M., *Victory and woe: the West Limerick Brigade in the War of Independence* (Dublin, 2002).
Harrington, N.C., *Kerry landing: an episode of the Civil War* (Dublin, 1992).
Hart, P., *The IRA and its enemies; violence and community in Cork 1916–1923* (Oxford, 1998).
— (ed.), *British Intelligence in Ireland: 1920–1921* (Cork, 2002).
Hopkinson, M., *Green against green: the Irish Civil War* (Dublin, 1988).
— (ed.), *Frank Henderson's Easter Rising: recollections of a Dublin Volunteer* (Cork, 1998).
— (ed.), *The last days of Dublin Castle: the diaries of Mark Sturgis* (Dublin, 1999).
—, *The Irish War of Independence* (Dublin, 2002).
Kiberd, D. (ed.), *Irish Times 1916 Rebellion handbook* (Dublin, 1998).
Kleinrichert, D., *Republican internment and the prison ship 'Argenta', 1922* (Dublin, 2001).
Kostick, C., *Revolution in Ireland: popular militancy 1917 to 1923* (London, 1996).
— and Collins, L., *The Easter Rising: a guide to Dublin in 1916* (Dublin, 2000).
Litton, H., *The Irish Civil War: an illustrated history* (Dublin, 1995).
MacEoin, U., *Survivors* (Dublin, 1981).
—, *The IRA in the twilight years, 1923–48* (Dublin, 1997).
McCoole, S., *Guns and chiffon: women revolutionaries and Kilmainham Jail, 1916–1923* (Dublin, 1997).
McDermott, J., *Northern divisions: the Old IRA and the Belfast pogroms, 1920–1922* (Belfast, 2001).

McGarry, F., *Frank Ryan* (Dundalk, 2002).
Murphy, J., *When youth was mine: a memoir of Kerry, 1902–1925* (Dingle, 1998).
Neligan, D., *The spy in the castle* (London, 1999).
Ní Chuilleanáin, E. (ed.), *'As I was among the captives': Joseph Campbell's prison diary, 1922–1923* (Cork, 2001).
Ó Corráin, D. (ed.), *James Hogan, revolutionary, historian, political scientist* (Dublin, 2001).
O'Drisceoil, D., *Peadar O'Donnell* (Cork, 2001).
Ó Duigneáin, P., *Linda Kearns: a revolutionary Irish woman* (Manorhamilton, 2003).
O'Farrell, M., *A walk through rebel Dublin in 1916* (Cork, 1999).
O'Farrell, P., *Who's who in the Irish War of Independence and Civil War, 1916–1923* (Dublin, 1997).
Ó Gadhra, N., *Civil war in Connaught, 1922–1923* (Dublin, 1999).
O'Mahony, S., *Frongoch: university of revolution* (Dublin, 1987).
O'Malley, E., *On another man's wound* (Dublin, 2002)
—, *The singing flame* (Dublin, 1978)
—, *Raids and rallies* (Dublin, 1982).
Regan, J.M., *The Irish counter-revolution, 1921–1936* (Dublin, 1999).
Stewart, A.T.Q., *The Ulster crisis* (Belfast, 1997).
— (ed.), *Michael Collins: the secret file* (Belfast, 1997).
Taillon, R., *When history was made: the women of 1916* (Belfast, 1996).
Townshend, C., *The British campaign in Ireland: the development of political and military policies* (Oxford, 1975).

THE SPANISH CIVIL WAR

Klaus, H.G. (ed.), *Strong words, brave deeds* (Dublin, 1994)
McGarry, F., *Irish politics and the Spanish Civil War* (Cork, 1999).
O'Riordan, M., *Connolly column* (Dublin, 1979)
Stradling, R., *The Irish and the Spanish Civil War* (Manchester, 1999).

THE SECOND WORLD WAR

Allen, T., *The storm passed by: Ireland and the battle of the Atlantic, 1940–41* (Dublin, 1996).
Barton, B., *Northern Ireland in the Second World War* (Belfast, 1995).
—, *The Blitz: Belfast in the war years* (Belfast, 1999).
Blake, J.W., *Northern Ireland in the Second World War* (Belfast, 2000).
Boyd, G., *Boyd's war: the story of a Royal Navy Volunteer Reserve fighter pilot during the Second World War* (Newtownards, 2002).

Doherty, R., *Clear the way: a history of the 38th (Irish) Brigade, 1941–1947* (Dublin, 1993).

—, *Wall of steel: the history of the 9th (Londonderry) HAA Regiment, Royal Artillery (8th)* (Limavady, 1988).

—, *Key to victory: the Maiden City in the Second World War* (Antrim, 1995).

—, *Irish men and women in the Second World War* (Dublin, 1999).

—, *Irish volunteers in the Second World War* (Dublin, 2001).

Doorly, M.R., *Hidden memories: the personal recollections of survivors and witnesses to the Holocaust living in Ireland* (Dublin, 1994).

Duggan, J.P., *Neutral Ireland and the Third Reich* (Dublin, 1989).

—, *Herr Hempel at the German legation in Dublin, 1937–1945* (Dublin, 2003).

Dunlop, E., *John Luke's Home Guard* (Ballymena, 1994).

Durney, J., *Far from the short grass: Kildare men in two world wars* (Kildare, 1999).

Dwyer, T. Ryle., *Guests of the nation: the story of Allied and Axis servicemen interned in Ireland during World War II* (Dingle, 1994).

Fleming, G., *Magennis VC: the story of Northern Ireland's only winner of the Victoria Cross* (Dublin, 1998).

Forde, F., *The long watch: the history of the Irish mercantile marine in World War Two* (Dublin, 2000).

Girvan, B. and Roberts, G. (eds), *Ireland and the Second World War: politics, society and remembrance* (Dublin, 2000)

Gray, T., *The lost years: the Emergency in Ireland, 1939–45* (London, 1997).

Gorman, J., *The times of my life* (Barnsley, 2002).

Gunner, C.J., *Front of the line: adventure with the Irish Brigade* (Antrim, 1991).

Hull, M., *Irish secrets: German espionage in wartime Ireland, 1939–1945* (Dublin, 2002).

Keefer, R., *Grounded in Éire: the story of the RAF flyers interned during World World War Two* (Montreal, 2001).

Kelly, M.P., *Home away from home: the Yanks in Ireland* (Belfast, 1994).

Litton, H., *The World War Two years: the Emergency in Ireland: an illustrated history* (Dublin, 2001).

McCarron, D., *'Step together!': Ireland's Emergency army, 1939–46 as told by its veterans* (Dublin, 1999).

—, *Landfall Ireland: Allied and German aircraft which came down in Éire in WW2* (Newtownards, 2003).

McCusker, B., *Castle Archdale and Fermanagh in World War Two* (Irvinestown, 2000).

McKeever, I. and McCarron, M., *The war years, Derry, 1939–45* (Derry, 1992).

Mawhinney, G. (ed.), *Toome's wartime airfield fifty years ago* (Draperstown, 1995).

Nolan, J., *Condition red: a west Belfast memoir of the German air raids of Easter Tuesday 7–8 April 1941 and Sunday 4–5 May 1941* (Belfast, 1999).

O'Donoghue, D., *Hitler's Irish voices* (Belfast, 1998).

Ó Drisceoil, D., *Censorship in Ireland, 1939–1945: neutrality, politics and society* (Cork, 1996).

O'Halpin, E. (ed.), *MI5 and Ireland, 1939–1945* (Dublin, 2002).

Quigley, M.S., *A US spy in Ireland* (Dublin, 1999).

Quinn, J., *Wings over the Foyle: a history of Limavady airfield in World War II* (Belfast, 1995).

—, *Covering the approaches, the war against the U-Boats: Limavady and Ballykelly's role in the battle of the Atlantic* (Coleraine, 1996).

—, *Down in a Free State: wartime air crashes in Éire, 1939–1945* (Belfast, 1999).

Redmond, S., *'Belfast is burning', 1941* (Dublin, 2002).

Robertson, D., *Deeds not words: Irish soldiers, sailors and airmen in two world wars* (Mullingar, 1998).

Ross, P., *All valiant lost: an Irishman abroad* (Dublin, 1992).

Tresdale, D., *Brotherhood of the cauldron* (Newtownards, 2003).

Walsh, R.R., *The Irish Guards roll of honour, 1939–1945* (Blackburn, 1999).

Wilson, I., *From Belfast Lough to D-Day* (Bangor, 1994).

Wood, I.S., *Ireland during the Second World War* (London, 2002).

THE IRISH DEFENCE FORCES

Brunicardi, D., *The seahound* (Dublin, 2001).

Duggan, J.P., *A history of the Irish army* (Dublin, 1991).

Harvey, D., *The barracks: a history of Victoria/Collins Barracks, Cork* (Cork, 1997).

—, *Peacekeepers: Irish soldiers in the Lebanon* (Dublin, 2001).

Gavin, J., *Military barracks, Dundalk: a brief history* (Dundalk, 1999).

MacDonald, H., *Irish Batt: the story of Ireland's Blue Berets in the Lebanon* (Dublin, 1993).

MacGinty, T., *The Irish navy: a story of courage and tenacity* (Tralee, 1995).

McCarron, D., *Wings over Ireland: the story of the Irish Air Corps* (Leicester, 1996).

—, *'Step together!': Ireland's Emergency Army, 1939–46 as told by its veterans* (Dublin, 1999).

McIvor, A., *A history of the Irish naval service* (Dublin, 1994).

Martin, K., *Irish army vehicles: transport and armour since 1922* (Dublin, 2002).

O'Shea, B. (ed.), *In the service of peace; memories of Lebanon* (Dublin, 2001).

Tormy, Comdt P. and Byrne, Capt K., *The Irish Air Corps: a view from the tower* (Dublin, 1991).

Military Heritage of Ireland Trust Limited

The Military Heritage of Ireland Trust Limited is a limited company, with charitable status, incorporated in June 2000. It is an all-Ireland organisation with directors from different traditions and a variety of backgrounds – business, public service and military.

The main object of the Trust is to promote a knowledge of the military heritage of Ireland, including its relationship to economic, political, social and cultural affairs, thereby fostering an appreciation of it.

The Trust sees the development of the Military Galleries in the National Museum of Ireland at Collins Barracks, Dublin, and the relocation of the Military Archives to that barracks, as key developments in promoting an awareness of the history of the Irish soldier. Together these will create a hub through which military museums and archives throughout Ireland can be linked and can co-operate in promoting our knowledge of our military heritage.

The trustees and staffs of the museums of The Inniskillings, the Royal Irish Fusiliers and The Royal Ulster Rifles co-operate with the Trust in supporting the development of those linkages. The Trust intends to establish similar links with other museums and archives in Ireland and in countries historically connected with the Irish soldier. Those developments, and the publication of this Guide, will assist in making the story of the Irish soldier accessible to all.

Ireland's military heritage is common to different political and religious traditions on this island and in the Irish diaspora. People of all traditions at home and abroad have come together in the study and commemoration of Irish men and woman who served in military forces on land, sea and in the air, regardless of their place of service or their cause.

DIRECTORS

P.F. Nowlan (Chairman), R.H. Bicker, J.J. Cullinane (USA),
W.H. Gibson, J.R. Gorman, K.C. McGoran, F. Murray, E.J. O'Halpin,
The O'Morchoe, P. Wallace, Maj. Gen. J. Sreenan (ex officio)

Index

Due to the high incidence of references to them in the guide, the following subjects, as such, do not appear in this index: 1798 Rebellion; 1916 Rising; World War One; World War Two.